DOGFIGHT 3

Bf 109D/E
Blitzkrieg 1939–40

Malcolm V. Lowe

OSPREY PUBLISHING
Bloomsbury Publishing Plc
Kemp House, Chawley Park, Cumnor Hill, Oxford, OX2 9PH, UK
29 Earlsfort Terrace, Dublin 2, Ireland
1385 Broadway, 5th Floor, New York, NY 10018, USA
E-mail; info@ospreypublishing.com
www.ospreypublishing.com

OSPREY is a trademark of Osprey Publishing Ltd

First published in Great Britain in 2022

A catalogue record for this book is available from the British
Library.

ISBN: PB 9781472850317; eBook 9781472850324;
ePDF 9781472850331; XML 9781472850348

22 23 24 25 26   10 9 8 7 6 5 4 3 2 1

Edited by Tony Holmes
Cover and battlescene artwork by Gareth Hector
Ribbon and technical diagrams by Tim Brown
Armament artwork by Jim Laurier
Maps by www.bounford.com
Index by Alan Rutter
Typeset by PDQ Digital Media Solutions, UK
Printed and bound in India by Replika Press Private Ltd

Osprey Publishing supports
the Woodland Trust, the UK's leading
woodland conservation charity.

To find out more about our authors and books visit
www.ospreypublishing.com. Here you will find extracts, author
interviews, details of forthcoming events and the option to sign
up for our newsletter.

Front Cover Artwork: The highest scoring *Jagdwaffe* pilot
during the Battle of France was Hauptmann Wilhelm Balthasar,
with claims for 23 victories. Already a veteran of aerial combat,
having served in Spain as a member of the *Legion Condor*, his
World War II scoring began with four claims on 11 May 1940
(three Belgian Gladiators and a French MS.406), and he
continued to enjoy success throughout the Battle of France.
Assigned to 1./JG 1, of which he was the *Staffelkapitän*, during
the course of a very busy period in early June, Balthasar
claimed five French victims on the 5th and a further four
the following day.

Previous Page: The winter of 1939–40 was particularly harsh.
Maintenance in the open was unpleasant and often dangerous.
This Bf 109E-1 with its very cold groundcrew belonged to
II./JG 77 based at Nordholz. (Author's Collection)

Acknowledgements The Author gratefully acknowledges help and
advice from historian friends and researchers, including
Heinz Björnson, Eddie J. Creek, Robert Forsyth, Marc-André
Haldimann, John Levesley, Siniša Sestanović, Jim Smith, Andy
Sweet, Peter Walter, John Weal, Wolfgang Witthain and Graham
Young. A special mention for the late John Batchelor MBE, whose
many years of research into the Luftwaffe and meetings with its
former personnel were a part of the background for this book.

Contents

CHAPTER 1
IN BATTLE

Although Britain and France had declared war on Germany on 3 September 1939, two days after the invasion of Poland had commenced, neither did anything directly to help the Poles. Therefore, the basing of several *Jagdwaffe* Bf 109 units in the western part of Germany to counter any possible intervention by British and French ground and aerial forces had been a wise but in the end unnecessary precaution. Instead, the RAF began smaller-scale operations against specific German military targets, most of these being raids across the North Sea aimed at naval ships and infrastructure of the *Kriegsmarine*. It was, therefore, only a matter of time before Luftwaffe and RAF aircraft met in combat. During these early encounters, the Luftwaffe's Bf 109s were often successful.

Oberstleutnant Carl-Alfred Schumacher was *Gruppenkommandeur* of Nordholz-based II./JG 77 at the start of World War II, his unit being tasked with defending maritime installations on the north German coast and Frisian Islands. (Tony Holmes Collection)

On 3 September an RAF Blenheim had spotted German naval forces in the Schillig Roads off Wilhelmshaven. A raid later that day failed to locate the intended targets, but on the 4th hostilities commenced in earnest. Further reconnaissance located German warships in the Schillig Roads, as well as off Brunsbüttel. The RAF sent a mixed force of Blenheim IV light bombers and Whitley and Wellington medium bombers in daylight to attack these targets. The different performance specifications and bombing capabilities of these diverse types was a bad combination in itself, but the strike force also had no fighter cover. It was a recipe for disaster.

To begin with, poor weather in the target area led to ineffective bombing results. Ready to meet the RAF aircraft was a group of Bf 109E fighters. Led by Oberstleutnant Carl-Alfred Schumacher, II./JG 77 was based at Nordholz and was tasked with local air defence for the various maritime installations along the nearby north German coastline and Frisian Islands. Schumacher was a veteran of World War I, during which he had served in the *Kaiserliche Marine* (Imperial German Navy) and saw action at the Battle of Jutland.

Alerted by ground observers to the presence of the RAF bombers, several of Schumacher's pilots rapidly became airborne. They soon intercepted the Wellingtons of No 9 Sqn, shooting down two in the first encounter of its kind during World War II. There has subsequently been debate as to which II./JG 77 member achieved the first victory. The two pilots concerned, Hans Troitzsch and Alfred Held, both held the rank of Feldwebel.

Troitzsch explained:

Former *Legion Condor* pilot Feldwebel Alfred Held of 6./JG 77 has been credited over the years with being the first Luftwaffe pilot to down an RAF aircraft (a Wellington from No 9 Sqn) in World War II. However, according to his *Gruppenkommandeur*, Major Carl-Alfred Schumacher, that accolade should have gone to Feldwebel Hans Troitzsch. (Tony Holmes Collection)

We were flying off the Elbe estuary when three English [bombers] came into view, flying low over the water. When we approached we saw they were twin-engined Wellington bombers. Two saw us, and at once flew towards the low cloud. I approached the third. When he was right ahead of me I closed to 100m to make certain that I could hit him. I began firing, and closed to 50m. His port wing broke up and fell away. Flames came out of the fuselage. I closed to 20m, but by then the bomber was engulfed in flames. The tail broke away and I was lucky because it passed just above my head. I dived to avoid the flames and then I followed him down.

The Wellington crashed into the water, leaving only a visible slick of oil.

At the same time (approximately 1815 hrs), Feldwebel Held had caught up with another Wellington. 'We strayed out over the Jade Bight when the English [bomber] dived to increase his speed and escape my fire', Held recalled. 'He was forced lower and lower. Suddenly flame shot from the left of the fuselage. He seemed to be out of control. One final burst from my guns was enough. The bomber dropped its nose and fell. I circled to watch its crash – there was a pile of burning debris on the water which disappeared in a few seconds.'

The Nazi propaganda machine swiftly made a hero of Feldwebel Held as the first ever victor over a British aircraft in World War II. However, Schumacher later wrote, 'I knew that Hansi Troitzsch's victory was the first. It was a big moment for us, and both pilots should have had the same fame placed on them.'

Somewhat ironically, Held did not live long enough to enjoy the accolade of being the first victor, whether it was correct or not. He was killed in a flying accident several days later on 17 September.

Wellingtons of RAF Bomber Command were amongst the first types of Allied aircraft downed by Bf 109 units defending the north German ports. Flying a series of unescorted attacks during daylight hours, both Wellington and Blenheim squadrons suffered terrible losses at the hands of the *Jagdwaffe*. This example was ditched in shallow waters off the Frisian Islands. (EN Archive)

In addition to the two victories of Held and Troitzsch, a third Wellington was credited to another pilot from II./JG 77. The vulnerability of the early Wellington IA with unprotected fuel tanks had been fully demonstrated. Four No 107 Sqn Blenheims were also shot down, with three falling to anti-aircraft fire from the shore and the fourth to Leutnant Metz of 4./JG 77.

On 29 September it was the turn of the Bf 109D pilots of I./ZG 26 to perform a successful interception, destroying five Hampdens of No 144 Sqn that were performing an armed reconnaissance, again without fighter cover.

The importance of the Bf 109 fighters in the defence of northern Germany and its maritime infrastructure thus ably demonstrated, Schumacher was later promoted to lead a properly integrated organisation combining Bf 109-equipped fighter units with a developing early warning infrastructure based around the ground-based *Freya* radar. This came under the umbrella of a newly created headquarters (*Stab*) organisation of JG 1 at Jever during November 1939, which Schumacher initially commanded as *Jafü Deutsche Bucht* (commander of fighters German Bight).

His replacement as the new leader of II./JG 77 was a pilot who would later become a well-known Bf 109 personality during the Battles of France and Britain, the veteran Major Harry von Bülow-Bothkamp. A fighter pilot in World War I, von Bülow-Bothkamp was an accomplished and respected leader who later became one of the *Jagdwaffe*'s most important *Geschwaderkommodore*.

Schumacher's north Germany command included amongst its ranks a variety of units, most equipped with the Bf 109. Several airfields including Jever and Wangerooge were employed, with short-lived units such as II.(J)/TrGr 186 and JGr 101 operating alongside II./JG 77 and I./ZG 26.

At the time the Bf 109 was increasingly regarded by the Luftwaffe's decision-makers as being not only the chief day fighter of the *Jagdwaffe*, but also a capable if austere makeshift nightfighter. Several ad hoc semi-autonomous nightfighter *Staffeln* eventually flew Jumo-engined examples of the type, sometimes alongside surviving Ar 68F biplanes. Amongst them was 10.(N)/JG 26, which for a time existed as a part of the north German defensive organisation. This *Staffel* was led by Oberleutnant Johannes Steinhoff who was to become a famous exponent of the Bf 109 later in the war and eventually an Me 262 pilot.

On 14 December the RAF attempted a daylight attack on the Leipzig-class light cruiser *Nürnberg* which had been disabled by a torpedo strike from a Royal Navy submarine. The north German *Freya* radar network detected the incoming Wellington bombers of No 99 Sqn, and several of the available Luftwaffe units were scrambled to intercept the formation. It was II./JG 77 that caught up with the bombers, and in the running battle that followed, five

Wellingtons were claimed by the Bf 109E pilots. Despite these losses, for little actual gain, the RAF persisted in this largely fruitless campaign, with a further raid mounted four days later. The ensuing encounter was the first named aerial event of World War II – the Battle of the Heligoland Bight.

Sometimes referred to as the 'Battle of the German Bight', the RAF pressed home an attack on Wilhelmshaven even though the weather was not ideal in being bright, with good visibility for defending fighters and little cloud cover for bombers under attack to hide in. The day's activity began when the incoming RAF bombers were detected by a part of the *Freya* radar chain. The RAF strike force consisted of 24 Wellington bombers from Nos 9, 37 and 149 Sqns. Two returned early to base, making a total of 22 Wellingtons that actually participated.

Only a small number of Bf 109s initially intercepted the bombers due to poor communication partly caused by some of the *Freya* stations being naval rather than Luftwaffe manned. The RAF formation flew over Wilhelmshaven intact, having only been engaged by surface and shipborne anti-aircraft fire. In this somewhat 'innocent' opening phase of the war, orders forbade the RAF aircrew from attacking warships in port for fear of inflicting civilian casualties. Only a small number of bombs were dropped, therefore, despite several potential targets being sighted.

By the time the Wellingtons departed the target area, Luftwaffe fighters were being scrambled and a major air battle ensued. The result was the loss of 12 bombers. Oberleutnant Steinhoff was amongst several pilots who achieved confirmed victories, giving the Bf 109D yet more laurels to its combat record. Other victors included Schumacher himself, and pilots of II./JG 77 flying from

The tail of Feldwebel Hans Troitzsch's Bf 109E Wk-Nr 1279 boasts three victory bars (all three for Wellingtons he had shot down in the early months of the war), two bullet patches dated 18/12/39 and the 6./JG 77 penguin insignia. (Tony Holmes Collection)

Jever accounted for several more. Recently arrived twin-engined Bf 110s were also fully involved in the ensuing dogfights. The Germans in fact originally claimed to have destroyed 38 bombers, which was far more than the attacking force. The Wellington gunners, however, were also successful, shooting down two Bf 109s with the loss of their pilots. Several others were wounded, including Feldwebel Hans Troitzsch who had been involved in the first shoot downs on 4 September.

An elated Oberstleutnant Schumacher explained:

> I saw two English [bombers] at a height of about 2,000 metres. I attacked at once, but without success. One of the Englishmen dived away, quickly dropping 1,000 metres or more, but my '109 was much faster. I was too fast, in fact, and my second pass was unsuccessful as well. So I throttled back, and on my third attempt I got onto his tail and fired my cannon and machine guns. I hit both of his engines. It was all over in a second and the English bomber crashed.

The overwhelming success of the German fighters on 18 December gave the Luftwaffe a somewhat inflated view of its own defences, while the RAF began to realise that lightly armed bombers operating in daylight without fighter cover were very vulnerable. It was an important step in the direction of the RAF adopting night-time strategic bombing for much of the rest of the war.

Somewhat appropriately, therefore, it was a significant advance when the various independent ad hoc Bf 109-operating nocturnal fighter units, including 10.(N)/JG 26, were amalgamated during February 1940 into a newly formed dedicated nightfighter *Gruppe* within JG 2. This was IV.(N)/JG 2, and it achieved its first success during the evening of 20 April when Oberfeldwebel Willi Schmale shot down an RAF Battle of No 218 Sqn while flying a Bf 109D. This was followed on the night of 25–26 April 1940 with the shoot down of a mine-laying Hampden (possibly from No 49 Sqn of Bomber Command) off the island of Sylt. These were the first victories by nightfighters over RAF bombers at dusk and at night – a further laurel for the Bf 109.

CHAPTER 2

SETTING THE SCENE

The first nine months of World War II were outstandingly successful for Germany's Luftwaffe. Several victorious campaigns, in which the aerial assets were a key component, endowed the Luftwaffe's aircrew and commanders with an air of invincibility. Beginning with the rapid defeat of Poland in September 1939 and continuing through to an equally comprehensive victory during the Battle of France in May–June 1940, the Luftwaffe literally swept aside the air opposition pitted against it.

Central to these overwhelming victories was the Bf 109 and the men who flew this outstanding fighter in combat. One of the great dogfighting machines in the history of aerial warfare, the Bf 109 is rightly regarded as an excellent example of a fast, manoeuvrable fighter, able to look after itself and successfully take on even its most capable contemporaries in aerial combat.

Bf 109 V1 Wk-Nr 758 performed its first flight in late May 1935 from Augsburg-Haunstetten airfield. At the controls was Messerschmitt's senior test pilot, Hans-Dietrich 'Bubi' Knoetzsch. The aircraft was powered by a 695hp Rolls-Royce Kestrel VI engine. Seemingly devoid of a pilot, the prototype was photographed during engine runs that preceded the first flight. (Tony Holmes Collection)

Conceived during the early 1930s and fully combat ready in September 1939 at the start of World War II, the Bf 109 was the Luftwaffe's only major single-seat warplane for the first two years of the conflict. By then it had been successfully combat-tested during the Spanish Civil War, which began in the summer of 1936 and witnessed the Bf 109 in combat with Germany's *Legion Condor* from the first half of 1937 onwards.

During the opening months of World War II, when flown by well-trained pilots, many of whom had experienced combat during the conflict in Spain, the Bf 109 proved to be a formidable opponent. This soon became obvious to the aircrew of several different countries who had to face these powerful and well-armed Luftwaffe fighters as the conflict widened. Added to this superiority were the developing organisation and tactics employed by Luftwaffe fighter units which placed them at an overwhelming advantage compared to the disorganised and tactically naive opposition that they regularly faced.

Legendary Luftwaffe fighter ace Generalleutnant Adolf Galland was in no doubt as to the usefulness of the Bf 109 during the opening months of World War II. Interviewed by the RAF's Air Historical Branch in 1953, he explained 'The Me 109 [sic] gave us a tool to take on and defeat the enemy ranged against us. The Me 109 not only possessed superior features, but it also caused a revolution in fighter design throughout the world.'

Veteran ace Generalleutnant Theodor Osterkamp, one of the Luftwaffe's 'Alter Hasen' (old hares) who had flown fighters with great success in World War I and was *Geschwaderkommodore* of JG 51 during 1940, later wrote, 'In the Me 109 [sic] we had a fighting machine that was better than our enemies. It gave us the edge.' Then-Major (and later Oberstleutnant) Carl-Alfred Schumacher, *Gruppenkommandeur* of II./JG 77, realised the importance of the Bf 109 in the overall context of the war. 'Our tactics were better, we learned from past mistakes. We knew how to fight with our machines, which were better than the enemy. Our enemies didn't understand this was real, total war.'

The accession to power of Adolf Hitler's National Socialists in Germany during early 1933, and with it the establishment of the Third Reich, had radically changed the shape and direction of the country's armed forces. Unprecedented rearmament, the introduction of advanced designs and a complete overhaul of institutions had resulted in a transformed military structure by the late 1930s. This affected not only ground and naval forces, but also the country's aerial assets, which by 1939 had become amongst the best in the world in terms of equipment, training and tactics.

The build-up of military aviation in Germany commenced very soon after the Nazis took power, allowing the Third Reich's new air ministry, the *Reichsluftfahrtministerium* (RLM), to begin formulating requirements for future warplanes through the auspices of its *Technisches Amt* (technical office). One of these specifications was for a modern single-seat monoplane fighter to improve on and replace existing biplanes. In meeting the various criteria that the RLM was looking for, the Bayerische Flugzeugwerke (BFW) of Munich subsequently created the basic design that led to the Bf 109. 'Willy' Messerschmitt and his talented designers and aerodynamicists produced a compact, nimble warplane with the manoeuvrability to make it, in the right hands, a great dogfighter.

The first prototype example made its maiden flight in late May 1935, in time for the new design to become a key element in the Third Reich's massive re-armament programme. Early production versions from the Bf 109B up to and including the Bf 109D were powered by the Junkers Jumo 210 inline engine. But from the Bf 109E onwards, excellent Daimler-Benz fighter engines were installed, starting with the DB 601A. This gave the Bf 109E the power to become a high-performance fighter, and its fuel-injection system allowed the type to manoeuvre in aerial combat at a considerable advantage compared to several of its potential adversaries.

The new Luftwaffe came into being during May 1933, but for a time its existence was kept as secretive as possible – Germany had been forbidden following World War I under the terms of the Treaty of Versailles to possess an air force capable of waging war. By the time that it was officially revealed in February 1935, the Luftwaffe was already a growing and increasingly menacing entity. Its fighter arm, or *Jagdwaffe*, was initially equipped with biplanes, of which the best was the He 51. But during 1937 the first examples of the Bf 109 in its Junkers Jumo-engined form began entering service.

Initial deliveries of Bf 109B production frontline fighters commenced to fighter wing JG 132 'Richthofen', its 1st *Gruppe* at Döberitz (in the Berlin area) and 2nd *Gruppe* at Jüterbog-Damm being selected as the first users. The latter in particular was tasked with assimilating the type into service, JG 132 being intended to develop tactics for the use of the new Messerschmitt fighter.

A neat line-up of brand-new Bf 109Bs, the first major production version of the Messerschmitt fighter line. The aircraft was arguably the most advanced fighter of its type in the world when it entered service with JG 132 'Richthofen' in March 1937. (Author's Collection)

However, events in Spain presented the Luftwaffe with the opportunity to test the Bf 109 in combat. The arrival in-theatre of Polikarpov I-15 and I-16 fighters from the Soviet Union for use by the legitimate Spanish government forces (Spanish Republicans) during the Civil War threatened to deny the skies to the anti-government Nationalists led by Gen Francisco Franco.

Following evaluation flights in Spain by four Bf 109 prototype/development airframes assigned to Germany's 'volunteer' *Legion Condor* from late 1936, initial examples of the Bf 109B were delivered in March 1937. They were the first of some 130 Bf 109s that were eventually assigned serial numbers prefixed with '6' for the aircraft's service in Spain, comprising examples of the Bf 109B, C, D and E. They served with the *Legion Condor's Jagdgruppe* 88 (J/88), which eventually comprised between three and four *Staffeln*. These units were at first equipped with He 51Bs, although the Heinkel biplanes were increasingly replaced in the fighter role by Bf 109s. J/88 also evaluated the He 112 (a Heinkel-built contemporary of the Bf 109) and Arado's Ar 68 nightfighter under operational conditions.

In Spanish skies, the Bf 109s were regularly pitted against Soviet Union-supplied combat aircraft, with the fighters that they encountered being predominantly I-16 'Rata' (rat) single-engined monoplanes. The Bf 109 proved to be an excellent fighter against these small and nimble warplanes, although on many occasions aerial combat turned into a free-for-all with little in the way of tactics or organisation. As a makeshift ground-attack platform the Bf 109 also operated with aplomb, this being an initial representation of the air-to-ground role for which later versions of the Bf 109 proved very useful in the following years.

Some 40 Bf 109s were lost to all causes during operations in Spain, with approximately 19 of them being shot down either by opposing Republican aircraft or by ground fire.

The Spanish Civil War ended on 1 April 1939. By that time there had been a considerable expansion in the number of domestic Luftwaffe units that had become operational in Germany with the Bf 109. It is often argued that the notorious 'Munich Agreement' of September 1938 bought time for Britain and France to continue re-arming, and that in particular it allowed the RAF to successively bring into service many more examples of the Hurricane and, eventually, the Spitfire. But in reality there is a completely different side to this argument. The avoidance of war in the autumn of 1938 was actually a great help to the Germans. It gave the Luftwaffe not only time to considerably expand its fighter force, it also allowed for a substantial reorganisation of the *Jagdwaffe* and the creation of many new fighter units.

At the command level for administrative and control purposes of Luftwaffe combat units, Germany was divided into three distinct areas each named a *Luftflottenkommando*. However, following the annexation of Czechoslovakia in March 1939 and the establishment of the 'Protectorate of Bohemia and Moravia', the original three districts were expanded into four during April of that year. These eventually took on the name *Luftflotte*. Within these overall umbrella organisations were various operational commands which controlled the fighters, bombers and other types allocated to each of the four *Luftflotten*.

A busy scene at La Sénia, in Spain, in the summer of 1938 as Bf 109s of 2.J/88 are prepared for another mission. Bf 109C-1 '6-60' in the foreground was an aircraft flown by Unteroffizier Herbert Schob. He ended World War II with 28 victories, having been awarded the Knight's Cross of the Iron Cross in June 1944 for his achievements as a *Zerstörer* pilot with ZG 76. The aircraft behind '6-60' has five victory bars on its rudder. (EN Archive)

In the northwest of Germany was *Luftflotte* 2, in the southwest and centre was *Luftflotte* 3, while *Luftflotte* 1 covered northeast Germany and the separate East Prussia, and, finally, the east/southeast of Germany and the annexed areas of the former Czechoslovakia were the responsibility of *Luftflotte* 4.

Allied with this major reorganisation were a number of changes to Luftwaffe frontline units. The old numbering system that had accompanied the birth of several of the premier fighter units was replaced by a simpler system. On 1 May 1939, the existing three-digit unit identification numbers were withdrawn in favour of a shorter numbering system. For *Luftflotte* 1, units were renumbered 1 to 25, whilst 25 to 50 was now used for *Luftflotte* 2, *Luftflotte* 3's assigned units were numbered 51 to 75, and 76 to 99 was delegated to units within *Luftflotte* 4.

Posed neatly for the camera, this Bf 109E-1 wears the *Gruppe* shield of I./JG 76 on its forward fuselage. This insignia featured the 'Lion of Aspern', which was a reference to the unit's Austrian ancestry. Formed on 1 May 1939 and operational during the *Blitzkrieg* period, the *Gruppe* was re-designated II./JG 54 in early July 1940 during a reorganisation of units prior to the aerial assault on Britain getting under way. (Author's Collection)

An example of this gradual transformation was displayed by JG 26, which was one of the principal fighter units that operated the Bf 109E during the early years of World War II. Indeed, this *Geschwader* became one of the leading Luftwaffe fighter wings of the conflict. The unit traced its origins back to the creation during March 1937 of I. and II. *Gruppe* of JG 234, which were equipped with the He 51 and Ar 68, respectively. On 1 November 1938 the *Stab* of a new unit, JG 132, was formed, and this absorbed the two *Gruppen* of JG 234. The major restructuring and renumbering of the Luftwaffe's fighter force during 1939 resulted in JG 132 becoming JG 26 on 1 May of that year – a title that it retained until the final days of World War II.

The first commander of JG 26 was Oberst Eduard Ritter von Schleich, whose *Stab* JG 26 (formerly the *Stab* of JG 132) was based at Düsseldorf. Its I. *Gruppe* (I./JG 26, formerly I./JG 132, led by Major Gotthard Handrick) was located at Köln-Ostheim, with II. *Gruppe* (II./JG 26, formerly II./JG 132, of Hauptmann Werner Palm) also at Düsseldorf.

JG 26 was one of the principal Luftwaffe fighter units from the start of the war, initially operating the Bf 109E-1. This meant it was one of the best-equipped *Jagdgeschwader* in the Luftwaffe at that time. It was also a prestigious 'named' unit, bearing the moniker 'Schlageter' in honour of Nazi folklore hero Albert Leo Schlageter who had been executed by the French on 26 May 1923 following his arrest for post-war sabotage against its occupation forces in western Germany.

The delay to the commencement of hostilities caused by the Munich Crisis additionally gained time for the Bf 109 to mature as a frontline fighter for the Luftwaffe. The original Jumo-engined Bf 109B of 1937 by then had been replaced in part by the Bf 109C and later in larger numbers by the Bf 109D, which was the best of the early versions of the Bf 109 family. But these were by no means 'the finished article', and if war had commenced during September 1938 the majority of the Luftwaffe's fighter force would have been Bf 109C/D-equipped.

However, during 1939, the more powerful Bf 109E began entering service in ever larger numbers, gradually replacing the 'Dora' as the main single-engined single-seat fighter in frontline service. This increasingly gave the Luftwaffe a huge leap forward in capability during the months following 'Munich'. Powered by the fuel-injected Daimler-Benz DB 601-series inline engine, the 'Emil' was a far more capable dogfighter and a formidable foe for any fighters of opposing nations that it was likely to meet in aerial combat.

Thus by the summer of 1939 the Luftwaffe was in significantly better shape to fight a major European war, both in terms of organisation and definitely with its increased capability, compared to the situation that existed the previous September at the time of 'Munich'. That war would begin with the intended attack on Poland.

In the event, a considerable amount of the Luftwaffe's strength was committed to the planning for the increasingly inevitable invasion of Poland, codenamed *Fall Weiss* (Case White or Plan White). However, the Germans suspected that the massive escalation of international tension that was certain to be occasioned by an attack on Poland would result not only in a declaration of war by Britain and France, but could also rapidly lead to actual intervention by the Western Allies. To that end, a sizeable part of the *Jagdwaffe*'s strength was concentrated prior to September 1939 in the western part of Germany, within *Luftflotten* 2 and 3. There were already a considerable number of air bases located in that part of Germany, with some airfields very close to the Belgian and Dutch borders.

In the same way that a large expansion of military airfields had been undertaken in Britain during the latter half of the 1930s, this had also been the case in Germany. Some of these 'permanent' air bases (*Fliegerhorste*) boasted excellent facilities, with considerable infrastructure of administrative buildings, hangars and maintenance facilities. Examples were to be found all over Germany, but in the western part of the country such airfields as Mannheim-Sandhofen were typical of the Luftwaffe's modern infrastructure.

A very large amount of money had been spent on building up the Luftwaffe in the years after 1933, and airfields were one very tangible and noticeable representation of this expenditure. It was certainly the boast of *Reichsmarschall* Hermann Göring, the *Oberbefehlshaber der Luftwaffe* (overall head of the Luftwaffe), that Germany's air force was the best in the world. In the dwindling peacetime days prior to the start of World War II, there were very few air forces anywhere that could match the Luftwaffe for its modern frontline and training equipment, infrastructure and organisation. It was the culmination of a great deal of hard work that had been carried out in the years following the Nazi accession to power in Germany during early 1933.

At the time of the commencement of the war against Poland on 1 September 1939, *Luftflotte* 1 was led by the very capable Albert Kesselring, *Luftflotte* 2 was headed by Hellmuth Felmy, *Luftflotte* 3 was the responsibility of Hugo Sperrle, and *Luftflotte* 4 was led by Alexander Löhr. All four held the rank of *General der Flieger* during that period.

The invasion of Poland was the first occasion in which the Luftwaffe's fighter force was able to display its prowess under its own colours. The successes of the *Legion Condor* in Spain had been achieved in aircraft adorned with markings that suited the situation in which German aircrew were 'volunteers' or on detachment helping Gen Franco's Spanish Nationalist forces. But over Poland the Luftwaffe had the opportunity to show its true potential wearing its own insignia.

The Bf 109s of *Luftflotte* 1 in the northeast of Germany and *Luftflotte* 4 in the east/southeast were committed to the forthcoming invasion. To that end, a number of these units began moving to forward bases in the days before the planned invasion. Some of the airfields used at that time were austere, and only existed for a short time. Similar to the Advanced Landing Grounds built and utilised by the Allies in Normandy during the weeks following D-Day in June 1944, they were only

One of a series of photographs taken at Biblis airfield in September 1939 of work being carried out on the Bf 109D-1 of Hauptmann Wilhelm-Otto Lessmann, who was then the *Gruppenkommandeur* of JGr 152 (I./ZG 52). Biblis was an excellently appointed operational airfield, with many of its buildings disguised to look like the traditional and substantial local Hessian half-timbered dwellings. Some of the airfield's buildings still stand today. (Author's Collection)

temporary installations. Such airfields as Lottin and Malzkow were little used following the Polish campaign and subsequently disappeared. However, others in eastern Germany, such as Gross Stein, were well appointed with good facilities for air- and groundcrews.

Although it was being increasingly replaced by the more powerful and workmanlike Bf 109E, the 'Dora' nevertheless played an important part in the fighter's overall operations during the Polish campaign. Flying alongside these Bf 109s were two-seat twin-engined Bf 110C *Zerstörer* heavy fighters, and both types were charged with escorting He 111 and Do 17 medium bombers and Ju 87 Stuka dive-bombers.

Opposing the aerial might of the Luftwaffe was the Polish Air Force, equipped with obsolete single-engined, fixed undercarriage PZL P.7 and P.11 high-wing monoplane fighters, single-engined PZL.23-series *Karaś* reconnaissance bombers and twin-engined PZL.37-scries *Łoś* medium bombers. None of these had the performance to seriously challenge the more modern German aircraft that they were likely to meet in combat. The Polish fighters were hardly numerous, with just 30 P.7s and 130 P.11s nominally available when the Wehrmacht invaded according to fragmentary Polish records. In comparison, the Luftwaffe could field approximately 400 Bf 109s of various marks, although not all of these were committed to the Polish campaign.

Following a 'false start' several days before, hostilities commenced on 1 September 1939. Immediately in action, the Luftwaffe was involved in preparing the way for ground forces by attacking vital targets at the commencement of what became known as *Blitzkrieg*, or lightning war. Indeed, the primary role of the Luftwaffe was to cooperate as far as possible with the army, helping to achieve rapid success on the ground. Only a comparatively small number of Bf 109-equipped units were needed for the Polish campaign, so comprehensive was the German attack in defeating the Polish aerial assets within days of the commencement of hostilities. They included I./JG 1, I./JG 21, I./JG 76, I./JG 77, JGr 102 (I./ZG 2), II./ZG 1, II.(J)/TrGr 186 and I.(J)/LG 2. Of these, *Trägergruppe* (TrGr) 186 was a complete anomaly, being

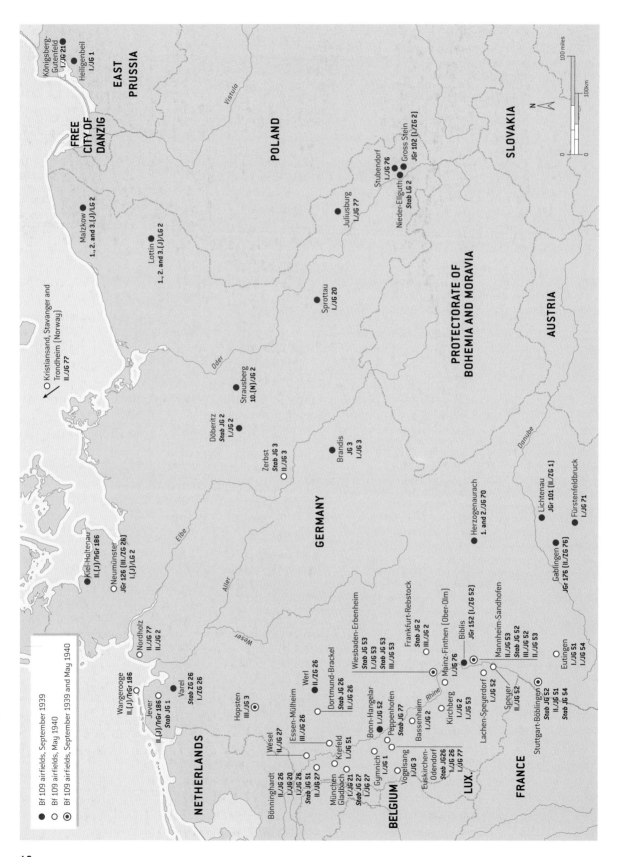

Königsberg-
Gutenfeld ●
I./JG 21
Heiligenbeil ●
I./JG 1

EAST
PRUSSIA

FREE
CITY OF
DANZIG

POLAND

Vistula

Malzkow ●
1., 2. and 3. (J)/LG 2

Lottin ●
1., 2. and 3. (J)/LG 2

Juliusburg ●
I./JG 77

Stubendorf ●
I./JG 76
Gross Stein ●
Jgr 102 (I./ZG 2)

Nieder-Ellguth
Stab LG 2

SLOVAKIA

N

100 miles

100km

Sprottau ●
I./JG 20

Strausberg ●
10. (N)/JG 2

Döberitz
Stab JG 2
I./JG 2 ●

Zerbst
Stab JG 3 ○
II./JG 3

Brandis ●
JG 3
I./JG 3

PROTECTORATE OF
BOHEMIA AND MORAVIA

Oder

AUSTRIA

Danube

Herzogenaurach ●
1. and 2./JG 70

Lichtenau ●
Jgr 101 (II./ZG 1)
Fürstenfeldbruck ●
I./JG 71

Kristiansand, Stavanger and
Trondheim (Norway)
II./JG 77

Kiel-Holtenau ●
II.(J)/TrGr 186
Neumünster ○
JGr 126 (II./ZG 26)
I.(J)/LG 2

Nordholz ○
II./JG 77
II./JG 2

Wangerooge
II.(J)/TrGr 186
Jever
II.(J)/TrGr 186 ○
Stab JG 1
Varel ●
Stab ZG 26
I./ZG 26

Hopsten ◉
III./JG 3

Elbe

Aller

Weser

GERMANY

Gablingen ●
JGr 176 (II./ZG 76)

Mannheim-Sandhofen ●
II./JG 53
Stab JG 52
III./JG 53
III./JG 53

Eutingen ○
I./JG 51
I./JG 54

Stuttgart-Böblingen ◉
Stab JG 52
I./JG 51
Stab JG 54

Bönninghardt
II./JG 26
I./JG 20
I./JG 26
Stab JG 51

München
Gladbach
I./JG 21
I./JG 27

Wesel
II./JG 27

Essen-Mülheim
III./JG 26

Dortmund-Brackel ●
Stab JG 26
II./JG 26

Werl ●
II./ZG 26

Wiesbaden-Erbenheim
Stab JG 53
I./JG 53
Stab JG 53
III./JG 53

Frankfurt-Rebstock
Stab JG 2
III./JG 2

Mainz-Finthen (Ober-Olm) ◉
I./JG 76

Bibilis ●
JGr 152 (I./ZG 52)

Krefeld ○
I./JG 51

Bonn-Hangelar ●
I./JG 52
Peppenhofen ◉
Stab JG 77

Gymnich ○
I./JG 1

Vogelsang ○
III./JG 3

Euskirchen-
Odendorf ○
Stab JG26
I./JG 26
I./JG 77

Bassenheim
I./JG 2

Kirchberg
I./JG 2
I./JG 53

Lachen-Speyerdorf ○
I./JG 52

Speyer ◉
II./JG 52

Rhine

LUX.

BELGIUM

NETHERLANDS

FRANCE

● Bf 109 airfields, September 1939
○ Bf 109 airfields, May 1940
◉ Bf 109 airfields, September 1939 and May 1940

Bf 109E-1 'Red 1' of 2./JG 77 provides the backdrop for Hauptmann Johannes Trautloft as he addresses groundcrew on the eve of the invasion of Poland. This *Staffel*'s *Gruppe* (I./JG 77) had been formed on 1 May 1939 as a part of the major reorganisation of fighter units that put the *Jagdwaffe* onto a war footing. Trautloft was one of many outstanding fighter pilots and unit commanders in the ranks of the *Jagdwaffe* during the early months of World War II. He was credited with five aerial victories in Spain, one during the Polish campaign and one during the Dunkirk evacuation. Trautloft would survive the war with at least 53 aerial victories to his name. (Author's Collection)

a *Gruppe* originally formed to operate from the planned *Kriegsmarine* aircraft carrier *Graf Zeppelin*.

The *Jagdwaffe*'s Bf 109 force committed to the campaign was in action straight away, with the fighter component of operational evaluation wing *Lehrgeschwader* (LG) 2 having the honour of being one of the first, if not the first, Bf 109 unit to see combat during World War II. Nevertheless, the earliest official aerial victory of the campaign, and therefore of World War II, was achieved by Ju 87B *Sturzkampfgeschwader* (StG) pilot Leutnant Frank Neubert of I./StG 2 flying from Nieder-Ellguth. He shot down a P.11 that tried to intercept his formation on the way home from an attack on the Polish airfield at Kraków during the morning of 1 September.

It was not until the following day that the Bf 109 units were able to engage successfully with Polish aircraft. Possibly the first victory was recorded by I.(J)/LG 2 when a short and successful dogfight took place between several of the unit's Bf 109Es and P.11 fighters. The German pilots claimed three of the totally out-gunned Polish warplanes.

The land invasion of Poland by the Wehrmacht proved to be very swift, necessitating that the Bf 109 units (and other Luftwaffe assets) follow the action by moving eastwards. This caused I.(J)/LG 2 to transfer from the temporary bases at Lottin and Malzkow to Lauenburg in Pomerania, northwest of Danzig, on 9 September. A further move followed, to an airfield in Poland itself north of Warsaw, until the *Gruppe* was withdrawn back to Germany, its work completed, on 20 September before the end of the Polish campaign.

Indeed, several of the Bf 109 units committed to supporting the invasion saw only infrequent aerial activity, with many (but not all) of the Polish aerial assets having been destroyed on the ground during the opening phases of the German attack. The comparatively small number of Polish fighters that were able to engage in aerial combat acquitted themselves very well, but that was almost entirely due to the skill and courage of their pilots rather than the quality of their aircraft.

As the invasion of Poland quickly gathered pace, the Bf 110 *Zerstörer* heavy fighters bore the brunt of the escort tasking for the various *Kampfgeschwader* (bomber wings) committed to the action. This freed up the Bf 109 pilots to undertake *freie Jagd* ('free hunt') operations looking for any serviceable Polish aircraft, and to assist when needed in performing ground-attack missions. The latter often comprised targets of opportunity when the Bf 109s stumbled upon some of the widely dispersed Polish aerial assets, many of which were well concealed on temporary landing grounds.

One of the Bf 109 units that did engage in aerial activity was I./JG 21, which had initially been formed during the summer of 1939 as an interim nightfighter unit with the Bf 109D. However, its role was soon changed to day fighter operations, still with the 'Dora', and as such the unit was based at Gutenfeld, in East Prussia, for the commencement of the Polish campaign.

On the opening day of hostilities, I./JG 21's Messerschmitts were tasked with bomber escort duties for He 111s ordered to bomb the Polish capital Warsaw. However, in a strange case of mistaken identity, the Heinkel gunners mistook the German fighters for Polish aircraft and opened fire. Fortunately for those involved, there were no fatalities on the German side. Instead, the 'Dora' pilots who stuck to their task encountered several P.11s and claimed four shot down.

Operating from Stubendorf, I./JG 76 achieved its first aerial victory of the campaign on 3 September. Conducting a *freie Jagd* sweep looking for Polish aircraft, several pilots of the unit's 1. *Staffel* encountered three PZL.23 *Karaś* apparently undertaking an armed reconnaissance and shot down one of them. This was only achieved when the much faster 'Emils' reverted to losing speed by deploying their wing flaps to match the slow-flying Polish aircraft. The victor was Leutnant Rudolf Ziegler, but return fire from the gunners in the Polish aircraft brought down the squadron's *Staffelkapitän*, Oberleutnant Dietrich 'Dieter' Hrabak. Making a forced landing behind the frontlines, Hrabak managed to avoid capture and later returned to the unit. He was, in subsequent years, to become a high-scoring fighter ace in the Luftwaffe and leader of two premier *Jagdgeschwader*.

Juliusburg was home to the 'Emils' of I./JG 77, which also had a varied, if limited, baptism to full-scale aerial warfare. The unit's first aerial victory came on 3 September, when future 75-victory ace Leutnant Karl-Gottfried Nordmann shot down a PZL.23 *Karaś* near Wieluń-Prosną. Like other *Jagdwaffe* pilots during the Polish campaign, he found it difficult to match the speed of his more powerful and faster Bf 109 to that of the slower Polish aircraft. Indeed, he overshot on his first attempt. Nordmann's *Katschmarek*, Leutnant Helmut Lohoff, then tried, but his *Rottenführer* wanted the kill for himself.

'I circled, avoiding our prey, and let Nordmann make a second attack', Lohoff explained. 'This time he came in with reduced speed, opening his landing flaps as well as lowering his landing gear. He only needed one volley of shots and the PZL.23 fell burning from the sky.'

Such a procedure, of losing momentum to manoeuvre at reduced speed by lowering not only the wing flaps but also the main undercarriage, was successful in this case. But it was definitely not to be found in the Messerschmitt's operating instructions. However, it was not the only time that a pilot resorted to these dangerous measures in order to ensure a shoot down. Flying slowly near to the Bf 109's stalling speed, especially in the vicinity of the ground with little chance of recovery, was definitely not a recommended combat manoeuvre – but apparently necessary under the circumstances. In this case it did demonstrate a trust in the Bf 109's flying capabilities that many pilots would nevertheless have refrained from trying for themselves.

Only three of the planned ten *Zerstörergruppen* were equipped with their intended new Bf 110C twin-engined heavy fighters by 1 September 1939. The others were flying a variety of Jumo-engined Bf 109s until sufficient Bf 110Cs were available. Five of them temporarily took on the title of *Jagdgruppe* for operations over Poland. Ironically, it was one of these transitory fighter units, Hauptmann Johannes Gentzen's JGr 102 (ex-I./ZG 2), that was the most successful Bf 109 *Gruppe* over Poland in terms of aerial victories. Gentzen himself was the top-scoring Bf 109 pilot during the Polish campaign, credited variously with seven or eight victories.

I./JG 77's first victory in Poland – a PZL.23 *Karaś*, downed near Wieluń-Prosną on 3 September 1939 – was claimed by future 75-victory ace Leutnant Karl-Gottfried Nordmann. He had to lower both the wing flaps and main undercarriage of his Bf 109E-1 in order to stay behind his considerably slower quarry. Cap on, he is seen here enjoying a celebratory drink upon returning to base at Juliusburg. (Tony Holmes Collection)

The direct ancestor of JGr 102 was created at Bernburg on 1 April 1936, initially as I./JG 232 with a mixed bag of biplane fighters including some He 51s. It went through a series of re-designations until, under the reorganisation of Luftwaffe units on 1 May 1939, the *Gruppe* became I./ZG 2. However, it temporarily reverted to the JGr 102 designation prior to the invasion of Poland. Based at Gross Stein, the unit marked its Bf 109Ds with the Bernburger Jäger ('Hunter of Bernburg') caricature on their fuselage sides in honour of where the *Gruppe* was formed.

The first day of the invasion consisted of an unopposed escort mission for Stuka dive-bombers, but 2 September was far more active for JGr 102. Gentzen was one of several pilots of the unit to shoot down a Polish aircraft, there being far more activity during this second 24-hour period of the campaign for his unit. Pilots of 1./JGr 102 discovered a concealed airfield at which they destroyed several parked Polish fighters by strafing, as well as shooting down several unidentified aircraft in aerial combat. Altogether JGr 102 as a whole was credited with 16 victories, including seven shot down, making it one of the most successful single tallies for a day's work amongst all the Bf 109 units committed to the Polish campaign.

JGr 102 pilots struggled to replicate the success of 2 September, for aerial opposition soon dwindled. 'The hardest part is tracking down the enemy fighters', Hauptmann Gentzen explained to a German war correspondent.

> The Pole is a master of concealment, and the olive-brown camouflage of his aircraft is an excellent colour scheme. Once found, bringing them down is quite a bit easier. Although, due to the superior speed of our machines, dogfights occur very seldom. Either you're in a good position and make one pass at high speed – preferably out of the sun – or you go off and hope to find a better target.

In order to keep pace with the Wehrmacht's advance on the ground, JGr 102 moved to Kraków, in southern Poland, and occasionally flew three of four missions per day, mainly supporting army units by strafing Polish ground

The Bf 109D-operating JGr 102 (I./ZG 2) was only intended as a temporary fighter unit while awaiting conversion onto the Bf 110C *Zerstörer*, but it emerged from the invasion of Poland as the top-scoring Luftwaffe fighter *Gruppe*. Its *Gruppenkommandeur*, Hauptmann Johannes Gentzen, was the campaign's only ace, and he is seen here sat in the cockpit of his 'Dora' in early September 1939. (EN Archive)

targets. However, the *Gruppe* achieved further success on 13–14 September by shooting down a handful of aircraft and destroying others while strafing an airfield in the east of the country where they had been gathered to escape the fighting. During the aerial encounter on 14 September Gentzen showed his fighting pedigree by shooting down four PZL.23s.

JGr 102 ended the Polish campaign with claims for 78 aircraft destroyed, 29 of these in aerial combat. The *Gruppe*'s Bf 109Ds had proven highly capable in this campaign, and JGr 102 emerged as by far the highest-scoring Luftwaffe unit following the Polish fighting.

Without doubt, sound planning, good equipment, experience from Spain and comparative weakness of opposition all culminated in the German victory over Poland. The intervention from the east by the Soviet Union on 17 September also helped to occasion the rapid Polish defeat, which was confirmed on 6 October 1939. Central to the German victory was the use of air power, and a vital component of the Luftwaffe's aerial activity was the Bf 109. Nothing that the Poles had been able to field against the Bf 109D/E units could stem the tide. Better tactics and weight of numbers had, of course, also been significant, as well as the fact that many Polish fighters had been prevented from joining combat following their destruction on the ground. But without doubt the superior design, firepower and performance of the Bf 109 gave the *Jagdwaffe* an overwhelming advantage in combat with the antiquated PZL fighters that were encountered over Poland.

In a historical context, the Polish campaign resulted in a quick and very efficient victory for Hitler's Germany, the ease of which shocked the watching world. However, the price was nevertheless relatively high for the Luftwaffe. Indeed, even though the Bf 109 did not play a central role in the operation, German records show that no fewer than 67 Bf 109s were lost to all causes during the campaign.

CHAPTER 3
PATH TO COMBAT

In German parlance the Luftwaffe fighter pilots were *Jagdflieger* – an elite group of flyers in the late 1930s and early 1940s. A considerable advantage enjoyed by the *Jagdwaffe* in the early months of World War II was not only good training. In comparison to the fighter pilots of the countries opposed to Nazi Germany, many of those flying Bf 109s were already experienced veterans due to their involvement in the Spanish Civil War while serving with the *Legion Condor*.

This cadre of pilots (and groundcrew) was invaluable for the Luftwaffe, as they had learned important tactical lessons due to their experiences while flying in combat over Spain. Many of the Spanish war veterans had engaged highly agile Soviet-built fighters with their fast, manoeuvrable Bf 109s, and had, in the process, gained important insights into battle formations.

Although *Reichsmarschall* Hermann Göring is often portrayed as being incompetent and without knowledge, he cannot be faulted in recognising the importance of having experienced personnel in the upper echelons of the new Luftwaffe of the post-1933 era. Göring had been a fighter pilot himself during World War I, and he was well aware of the importance of experience and know-how. To that end the Luftwaffe of the late 1930s and early 1940s had a considerable cadre of knowledgeable and competent pilots in the frontline, often as high-ranking officers in the large number of new fighter units that were being formed. Several of these pilots were also combat veterans from World War I, and were considerably older than the newly qualified but well-trained *Jagdflieger* who were joining the Luftwaffe's fighter units from pilot training in the late 1930s. Interestingly, however, it was the bomber crews who were considered, at the start of World War II, to be the Luftwaffe's most important flying personnel.

Among the officers who traced their military careers back to World War I was Theodor 'Theo' Osterkamp. Born in the Kingdom of Prussia on 15 April 1892, he was of military age on the outbreak of war in August 1914, and performed his pilot training with the naval air arm of Imperial Germany's *Kaiserliche Marine*. After a spell as an observer in two-seaters, Osterkamp entered training as a fighter pilot in March 1917. Having graduated, he remained in combat

until the end of the war, flying amongst other types the iconic Fokker D VII biplane fighter. Osterkamp ended the war with a tally of 32 aerial victories to his name, making him the highest-scoring German naval pilot of the war. He was awarded the prestigious *Pour le Mérite* or 'Blue Max' award on 2 September 1918, having already received the *Eisernes Kreuz I. Klasse* (Iron Cross First Class).

Post-war, Osterkamp flew in combat with the '*Kampfgeschwader* Sachsenberg' during the local war to halt Bolshevik incursions into Courland (part of present-day Latvia) in 1919, before returning to civilian life.

Answering the call to join the newly constituted Luftwaffe during the summer of 1933, Hauptmann Osterkamp served in a number of increasingly important command positions, initially with He 51B-equipped JG 132 and then with the rank of Major as *Gruppenkommandeur* of Werl-based II./JG 134 from March 1936, flying the Ar 68E. This unit began re-equipping with the Bf 109B later in 1937, which was Osterkamp's first association with the type.

From November 1937 until November 1939, he was the commanding officer of the fighter training school *Jagdfliegerschule Werneuchen* (later designated JFS 1). However, upon the outbreak of war, Oberstleutnant Osterkamp was at once given a significant posting as *Geschwaderkommodore* of premier Bf 109E unit JG 51, which was brought up to full *Geschwader* strength by the creation of its *Stab* on 25 November 1939 at Münster-Handorf. This was the third of five *Geschwader* that were thus elevated to full organisational and operational strength during the 'Phoney War' period. It was pre-dated in that respect by JG 27 and JG 77, and was followed by JG 1 and JG 54.

Osterkamp now held the rank of Oberst, and at 47 years of age was certainly a senior commander. Known as 'Onkel Theo' (Uncle Theo) to those who he commanded, he was a well-liked senior officer whose pedigree as a fighter pilot and leader could not be doubted. He presided over JG 51 during its participation in the *Sitzkrieg* on the 'western front', during which time the unit only encountered sporadic action. However, his *Geschwader* was fully involved from the first day onwards of the German invasion of the Low Countries and France on 10 May 1940.

Osterkamp led from the front, with the units under his command committed to supporting ground and air echelons spearheading the assault on the Netherlands and Belgium. It was during this period that he began adding to his list of aerial kills that dated back to World War I. As *Geschwaderkommodore* of JG 51, and found himself in action against Dutch fighters and ground-attack aircraft. On 12 May he was credited with shooting down a twin-engined, twin-boom Fokker G.1 that was strafing a German troop column advancing along the Arnhem–Amsterdam road:

I eased gently down through a layer of cloud. Nothing to be seen. Why I chose to look down and behind me to the left I don't know, but suddenly – there! – I catch a glimpse of something. Now it's gone again. Ease off the throttle and get down lower. Perhaps from ground level I can spot him against the light of the western sky. I'm now at tree-top height. And there, off to the right, not a thousand metres ahead of me, the devil. But he's fast – full throttle and after him. He obviously hasn't seen me. He's flying straight and level at a height of some 200m. I begin to catch up on him, closer and closer. I'm soaked in sweat and can hardly see through my dark sunglasses for the condensation.

A twin-boom fighter, its Dutch markings clearly visible. Now I'm just behind and below him, pull the nose up slightly – he's filling my sights – and press all four gun buttons. All I can see are pieces flying off him. He rears up to the left and then plunges into the ground like a comet. My God, is that it? I feel he ought to still be in front of me – I had hardly fired a round. I circle. There, in the hedge alongside the road, a heap of debris, and more strewn all over the countryside – a wheel here, an engine there, and bits of wing and fuselage. When I think of the last war, coming back to base on one occasion with 'only' 68 bullet holes in my bird. A quick canvas patch, with a roundel and a date painted on each, and then it was back up into the fray again. But today, one hit and it's all over. We're using 'cannons to shoot at sparrows!'

In the following weeks Osterkamp claimed three Hurricanes destroyed in the Dunkirk area, although these successes were unconfirmed. His final victory came on 13 July, when he was credited with downing a Spitfire off Dover. Osterkamp continued at the head of JG 51 until replaced by his long-standing colleague Major Werner Mölders one week later, by which time the Battle of Britain had commenced. He briefly resumed command when Mölders was wounded on the 28th of that month. Duly promoted to Generalmajor, Osterkamp was awarded the prestigious Knight's Cross (*Ritterkreuz*) of the Iron Cross on 22 August 1940 and was promoted as the *Jagdfliegerführer* of the fighter units in *Luftflotte* 2 during the Battle of Britain.

Generalmajor Theo Osterkamp congratulates Major Werner Mölders shortly after the latter had achieved his 50th victory of World War II on 29 October 1940. By now Osterkamp was serving as *Jagdfliegerführer* of the fighter units in *Luftflotte* 2. Standing in the centre of the photograph is Hauptmann Walter Oesau, then the *Gruppenkommandeur* of III./JG 51. Like Mölders, Oesau was also a *Legion Condor* ace and a highly successful Bf 109E pilot during the Battles of France and Britain. (Tony Holmes Collection)

One of the high-ranking combat pilots that were a feature of the Luftwaffe during the opening months of World War II was Oberstleutnant Harry von Bülow-Bothkamp, who became *Geschwaderkommodore* of JG 2 'Richthofen' on 1 April 1940. A fighter pilot during World War I, von Bülow-Bothkamp was one of several German aviators who flew in both conflicts. (Tony Holmes Collection)

In subsequent years he held several further senior appointments, but was removed from these duties during 1944 when he fell out of favour. Never an ardent Nazi, Osterkamp was later taken into custody by the Allies at the end of World War II and interned briefly in England. He passed away in Baden-Baden, West Germany, on 2 January 1975, aged 82.

Another veteran of World War I who successfully flew the Bf 109E during the early stages of World War II was Harry von Bülow-Bothkamp. He was a member of the noble Bülow family, which dated back to the 1200s and owned a number of ancestral estates in northern Germany. Born on 19 November 1897 at his family's castle in Bothcamp, Schleswig-Holstein, von Bülow-Bothkamp was one of four brothers. All four fought in World War I, but he was the only one to survive the conflict. He joined the *Luftstreitkräfte* (Imperial German Air Service) in December 1916 and eventually flew as a member of *Jagdstaffel* (*Jasta*) 36, a fighter unit that was commanded by his brother Walter. Von Bülow-Bothkamp was awarded the Iron Cross, First Class, in May 1917, and finished the war with six confirmed victories. His brother Walter was killed in action during January 1918, having by then taken command of *Jasta* 2.

Harry von Bülow-Bothkamp joined the nascent Luftwaffe in 1935 with the rank of Hauptmann, and gradually worked upwards through the ranks of the *Jagdflieger*, becoming *Gruppenkommandeur* of Bf 109E-equipped II./JG 77 at the end of November 1939 with the rank of Major while the unit was moving temporarily to Gütersloh. Fully involved in the 'Phoney War', the *Gruppe* was stationed more permanently at Jever until March 1940, and it was eventually located in Norway for much of the rest of 1940 following the Norwegian campaign.

By then, however, von Bülow-Bothkamp had moved on to the prestigious post of *Geschwaderkommodore* for Bf 109E-equipped JG 2 'Richthofen', which was one of the premier 'named' *Geschwader* of the Luftwaffe. He took this post on 1 April 1940 at the age of 42, replacing Oberst Gerd von Massow, who had led the *Geschwader* since it was formed on 1 May 1939. Harry von Bülow-Bothkamp duly commanded the unit throughout the Battle of France, during the brief summer break and then in the Battle of Britain, by which point he had attained the rank of Oberstleutnant. He was replaced as the leader of JG 2 in early September 1940 by Major Wolfgang Schellmann, having claimed 12 victories in the Bf 109E, although this total is disputed in some claims summaries. What is certain is that he achieved more than five victories during the *Blitzkrieg* period, making him one of the very few aviators who gained ace status during both World Wars.

Behind the scenes, a reason for both von Bülow-Bothkamp and Theo Osterkamp being removed from their combat status was the excuse that *Reichsmarschall* Göring was developing to justify the failure of the Luftwaffe's campaign in the Battle of Britain. The *Führer* was being told that the lack of overall success was due to the older commanders doing badly and losing their

Preparing for a mission during the early stages of the Battle of Britain, Oberstleutnant Harry von Bülow-Bothkamp gets a helping hand with his kapok lifejacket and flare pistol. His Bf 109E-3 has been the subject of 'in-the-field' camouflaging, with its previously pristine pale Hellblau surfaces darkened with hand-applied dense dappling. (Author's Collection)

way. Of course this statement was baseless, and it was ironic that Göring had had pilots such as these promoted to high office in frontline units in the first place due to their undoubted knowledge and combat experience. In a further ironic twist, von Bülow-Bothkamp had been awarded, just days earlier on 22 August, the Knight's Cross of the Iron Cross for his exceptional leadership.

Following his time as leader of JG 2, von Bülow-Bothkamp held several other command and staff positions, latterly as a part of the increasingly hard-pressed Defence of the Reich organisation during 1944. Like a number of other experienced senior officers, he played little part in the pursuit of the war from the latter half of 1944 onwards. Von Bülow-Bothkamp eventually passed away on 27 February 1976, aged 78.

These two veteran pilots illustrate the fighting prowess of the German airmen from both wars, and the fact that the Bf 109E gave them an exceptional machine with which to pursue for the second time in their lives the aerial warfare that they excelled at. Although most *Jagdflieger* were younger and less-seasoned pilots than Osterkamp and von Bülow-Bothkamp, they were no less accomplished when it came to tactics and flying skills. One of Theo Osterkamp's friends and colleagues from the mid-1930s was a Bf 109 pilot who would rise to rapid fame and very considerable accomplishment – the celebrated Werner Mölders.

Born on 18 March 1913 in Gelsenkirchen, Mölders joined the Luftwaffe during March 1934, having already undergone army military training in the *Reichswehr* (the Weimar Republic's armed forces) during 1931. His flying training commenced in Cottbus, where, initially, he showed little promise as a student. He eventually moved to the advanced fighter pilot training establishment *Jagdfliegerschule Schleissheim* near Munich. With the rank of Leutnant, Mölders gained his 'wings' during May 1935. His most important early posting was to II./JG 134 at Werl in the spring of 1936, with a promotion

Hauptmann Werner Mölders, *Staffelkapitän* of 3.J/88, stands in front of his Bf 109D-1, coded '6-79', which carried the name *Luchs* (Lynx) on both sides of the engine cowling. Mölders would emerge as the highest scoring German pilot in Spain by the end of the Civil War with 14 victories. (EN Archive)

to Oberleutnant. There, he became acquainted with the *Gruppe*'s commander, Theo Osterkamp, who was to be a considerable and very positive influence on his development as a fighter pilot.

On 15 March 1937 JG 334 was created, with its I. *Gruppe* based initially at Mannheim-Sandhofen. Mölders became *Staffelkapitän* of 1./JG 334, this unit initially being equipped with the Ar 68E. Later that year, I./JG 334 started to convert to the Bf 109B, giving Mölders his first real acquaintance with the type that he was soon to fly so successfully in combat. He then spent some time as an instructor to trainee fighter pilots.

By that time the Spanish Civil War had already commenced, and Mölders volunteered for service there as a member of the *Legion Condor*'s J/88. In the event, he arrived in Spain comparatively late in the conflict, but he was very quickly to demonstrate his mastery of the Bf 109 and its fighting qualities. Upon joining J/88 in April 1938, he was allocated to 3. *Staffel*, which at the time was still flying He 51Bs principally on ground-attack missions. The Heinkel biplanes had been withdrawn from the fighter role due to them becoming increasingly outclassed by Spanish Republican I-15s and I-16s supplied by the Soviet Union.

The *Staffel* was commanded by Leutnant Adolf Galland, although Mölders took over as *Staffelkapitän* when the former returned to Germany towards the end of the following month. The unit soon began conversion onto the Bf 109, and during an exceptional spell of just over six months, Mölders displayed both his excellent mastery of the type and his profound understanding of the need for proper fighter tactics.

Usually flying a Bf 109D-1 coded 6-79, he achieved his first success on 15 July 1938 when he shot down a I-15 'Chato' – this aircraft was identified as a 'Curtiss' by the future ace. Thereafter, Mölders scored with regularity, claiming his 14th, and last, victory on 3 November 1938. The 14 victories (11 of them I-16s) made him the highest-scoring German pilot in Spain, ahead of Hauptmann Wolfgang Schellmann (12 victories) and Hauptmann Harro Harder (11 victories), both of 1.J/88.

Mölders had quickly recognised the importance of the two-aircraft *Rotte* and duly flew with a wingman, usually Unteroffizier Franz Jaenisch, while also developing the concept of the four-aircraft *Schwarm*, which was to become so important to Luftwaffe tactics in World War II.

Returning to Germany in early December 1938, having been promoted to Hauptmann two months earlier, Mölders was posted to I./JG 133 and eventually became its *Staffelkapitän*. This *Geschwader* was the successor to JG 334, which he had previously flown with, and on 1 May 1939 it was renumbered as JG 53. The unit was to become synonymous with the Mölders name. Based at Wiesbaden-Erbenheim, JG 53 was one of the Bf 109E-equipped units tasked with the defence of the western border of Germany.

For a part of that time, Mölders was delegated to a staff position in the department of the *Inspekteur der Jagdflieger* in Berlin. While there, he was one of several experienced officers who were tasked with devising new fighter tactics based on knowledge of the air war in Spain that would bring out the best fighting qualities and performance capabilities of the Bf 109.

Upon the outbreak of World War II, JG 53 remained in the west with its Bf 109Es, awaiting a feared attack on land and in the air from Britain and France, which in reality did not come. Instead, the unit settled down into being one of the participants of the 'Phoney War'. During the early days of the conflict, Mölders suffered a potentially serious accident. On 8 September his Messerschmitt was damaged during an inconclusive encounter with French fighters causing an engine failure, forcing him to make a crash landing. The aircraft turned over, leaving him with back injuries that prevented him from flying until 19 September, although he was fortunate to escape from the incident without greater harm.

On the 20th, his *Schwarm* became involved in a full-on aerial battle over the *Dreiländereck* ('three borders') area, where Germany, Belgium and the Netherlands meet, with French Curtiss Hawk H-75s of GC II/5 while he was flying with I./JG 53:

> I took off with my *Schwarm* at 1427 hrs to intercept six enemy monoplanes reported south of Trier. As the *Schwarm* overflew the Saar River near Merzig at 4,500m, six machines were sighted south of Contz [Contz-les-Bains] at 5,000m. I climbed above the enemy in a wide curve to the north and carried out a surprise attack on the rearmost machine. I opened fire from approximately 50m, whereupon the Curtiss began to fishtail. After a further lengthy burst, smoke came out of the machine and individual pieces flew off it. It then tipped forward into a dive and I lost sight of it, as I had to defend myself against other opponents newly arriving on the scene.

Mölders' first successful combat of World War II represented the classic 'bounce' manoeuvre, whereby superior height and the element of surprise were the main advantages. His next victory, on 30 October, proved to be somewhat easier. By then, the 'Phoney War' was becoming well established,

Newly promoted Major Werner Mölders converses with his groundcrew from the cockpit of his Bf 109E-3 in late July 1940, having only just been made *Kommodore* of JG 51. He was wounded fighting with Spitfires from No 41 Sqn over the Channel on 28 July, Mölders having to force-land his Messerschmitt at Saint-Inglevert in the Pas-de-Calais. He was subsequently hospitalised in Berlin for ten days following this close shave. (Tony Holmes Collection)

and RAF reconnaissance aircraft were routinely being engaged by Bf 109 pilots patrolling the 'western front'. Writing for *Der Adler*, Mölders described his encounter with an RAF Blenheim I of No 18 Sqn on this date:

> I took off with the *Gruppenschwarm* and three *Schwärme* of 9. *Staffel* [of JG 53] for a patrol to counter enemy reconnaissance aircraft in the Bitburg–Merzig area. At 1112 hrs I noticed Flak activity near Trier. I approached to within 50m of the enemy aircraft without being seen, and saw the British roundel very clearly. I opened fire and closed to the shortest possible range without any return fire from the rear gunner, and the left engine gave out a thick white cloud of smoke. It changed very quickly to black. When I pulled up beside it, the aircraft was totally on fire. I observed a parachute, but it seemed to kindle.

In late October/early November III./JG 53 was formed at Wiesbaden-Erbenheim, and Mölders became its *Gruppenkommandeur*. It was a post that he would hold until early June 1940. Further success followed. On 22 December, Mölders was leading a *Schwarm* of Bf 109Es from III./JG 53 when they sighted and bounced three Hurricanes from No 73 Sqn over the Saar River, near Metz. Mölders and Oberleutnent Hans von Hahn each shot one down, thus becoming the first German fighter pilots to destroy Hurricanes during the war.

Mölders subsequently reported, 'I shot at the aircraft on the left. It began to "swim" immediately – I must have hit the pilot. The aircraft burned, and crashed close to a village.' Fellow future ace von Hahn was a little more effusive in his account of the action:

I remembered the orders of 'Vati' Mölders to 'go up to the enemy and sit up straight behind the gunsight'. Then I pushed the gun button, the Hurricane went into a slight turn and just at that moment it was hit by a cannon shell under the cabin. My burst must have hit the pilot. The Hurricane tipped over, a blast of flame, and like a fiery comet the aircraft crashed down.

Mölders continued to achieve successes during the 'Phoney War', receiving the Iron Cross First Class in April 1940, so that by the time of the *Fall Gelb* (Case Yellow or Plan Yellow) attack on the Low Countries and France on 10 May 1940, he had claims for nine Allied aircraft. JG 53 was involved from the start of the *Blitzkrieg* in the West, but on 14 May Mölders was shot down while engaging enemy bombers in the Sedan area, successfully bailing out of his stricken aircraft. On 29 May he was the first Luftwaffe *Jagdflieger* to be awarded the Knight's Cross of the Iron Cross.

CLASH OF ACES

One of the stars of the *Jagdwaffe* during the early months of World War II was Hauptmann Werner Mölders, who was instrumental in developing tactics for modern aerial fighting. He rose to become the *Gruppenkommandeur* of III./JG 53 in late October/early November 1939, and was the second highest-scoring Luftwaffe *Experte* during the Battle of France. However, on 5 June 1940, in a dogfight with *Armée de l'Air* D.520s (which he mis-identified as MS.406s), he became the fifth victim of Sous-lieutenant René Pomier-Layrargues from GC II/7. Mölders later wrote:

'Beneath me, two Messerschmitts are still having a go at the last Morane.

'I watch the fight for a while and then go in to attack a Morane which is being chased – without success – by three other Messerschmitts. I soon have him in my sights – he immediately dives away, but clearly hasn't had enough yet. Suddenly, he pulls up beneath me, I lose sight of him underneath my wing – there he is again, below me off to one side – *Donnerwetter!* This Morane can shoot too, although he's well wide of the mark.

'I bank away and climb up into the sun. He must have lost me, for he banks in the opposite direction and disappears to the south. Beneath me, two Messerschmitts are still having a go at the last Morane.

'A glance above and behind me – the sky is still full of weaving Me's. I am at about 800m, when suddenly there is a bang and the sparks fly across the cockpit. The throttle is shot to pieces, the stick flops forward. I'm going down vertically. Got to get out, otherwise it's all over. I grab the jettison lever and the canopy flies off. My faithful bird points her nose upwards for a second or two and gives me one last chance to undo my harness and clamber out of the seat. Free!'

Mölders duly parachuted to safety, but was quickly captured and spent the final days of the Battle of France as a PoW until he was released as a result of the Armistice which signalled the defeat of France. His victor, Pomier-Layrargues, who then reportedly destroyed a second Bf 109, was himself shot down in flames by another 'Emil' just moments after despatching Mölders.

FOLLOWING PAGES

Mölders was shot down again on 5 June when elements of JG 53 were engaged in combat by the best of the French fighters of that era, the Dewoitine D.520. He and his *Stabsschwarm* were about to attack a formation of six 'Moranes' near Compiègne when another *Staffel* from III./JG 53 dived in front of them. The latter then opened fire much too early, alerting the French fighters, who immediately broke in all directions. A wild dogfight developed and Mölders was eventually shot down.

He had become the fifth victim of Sous-lieutenant René Pomier-Layrargues from GC II/7, who then reportedly downed a second Bf 109 before he was himself shot down in flames moments later. Mölders was captured by French soldiers upon reaching the ground, and he spent three weeks as a Prisoner of War (PoW) until freed by the Armistice that ended the hostilities in France. He subsequently returned to Germany and was promoted to Major on 19 July 1940. Several days later Mölders took command of JG 51 from his old mentor Theo Osterkamp. By then the Battle of Britain was in progress, and flying a combat mission on 28 July, he was wounded while dogfighting with RAF Spitfires and forced to make an emergency landing in France. While Mölders was recuperating, Osterkamp temporarily took back command of JG 51.

Returning to the frontline, Mölders added to his score of aerial victories, claiming some 28 RAF fighters during the remainder of the Battle of Britain. On 22 October he downed three Hurricanes to become the first Luftwaffe pilot to reach 50 aerial victories. By the end of the Battle of Britain his score stood at 54, and he had risen to the rank of Oberstleutnant. Virtually all of these victories had been claimed while flying Bf 109Es.

As one of the Luftwaffe's most esteemed fighter pilots, Mölders was given the opportunity to fly examples of both the Hurricane and Spitfire at the *Erprobungsstelle* (testing establishment) at Rechlin in early 1941 He subsequently commented:

> It was very interesting to carry out the flight trials with the Spitfire and the Hurricane. Both types are very simple to fly compared with our aircraft, and childishly easy to take-off and land. The Hurricane is good-natured and turns well, but its performance is decidedly inferior to that of the Bf 109. It has strong stick forces and is lazy on the ailerons. The Spitfire is one class better. It handles well, is light on the controls, faultless on the turn and has a performance approaching that of the Bf 109.

Mölders continued flying in combat over the Channel Front into the early months of 1941, but the emphasis of the war was about to dramatically change and JG 51 was relocated east. The unit by then had been actively converting onto the new Bf 109F. On 22 June 1941, the first day of Operation *Barbarossa* on what became the new Eastern Front,

Generally regarded as one of the *Jagdwaffe*'s master tacticians, Werner Mölders was a well-respected and popular leader whose piloting and dogfighting skills could not be questioned. He was a significant participant in the development of fighter tactics that were so successful for the *Jagdwaffe* during the *Blitzkrieg* period, and many of these aspects of air combat are still of relevance today. His untimely death in a flying accident on 22 November 1941 was a major blow to the *Jagdflieger*. (Author's Collection)

Mölders shot down four Soviet aircraft. He was the first German pilot to surpass Manfred von Richthofen's World War I record score of 80 aerial victories on 30 June, when he was credited with five SB-2 light bombers destroyed. During the course of that day JG 51 claimed more than 95 Soviet aircraft shot down. On 15 July Mölders became the first pilot in history to record 100 aerial victories. He was immediately forbidden to fly further combat missions on the personal orders of Göring himself.

Mölders was now the star of the Luftwaffe's *Jagdflieger*, and their leading *Experte* (ace). Celebrated and well liked, he was known to many by the nickname 'Vati' ('daddy'). At only 28 years of age, he was promoted to Oberst and appointed *Inspekteur der Jagdflieger* in early August. Even though ordered to cease flying combat missions, he continued to do so, and is reputed to have achieved several unconfirmed victories over the Crimea.

However, on 22 November 1941, he was a passenger in a He 111 that was travelling from the Crimea so that he could attend the funeral in Berlin of Luftwaffe procurement chief Generaloberst Ernst Udet, who had committed suicide several days earlier. Whilst attempting to land in a thunderstorm at Breslau, the aircraft crashed. Of the He 111's five occupants, three perished, including Mölders. It has since been speculated that if he had been wearing a seatbelt he would have survived the accident.

In an unrivalled combat career, Mölders had flown approximately 330 combat sorties during World War II, eventually finishing with a score of 101 aerial victories to his name. All of these were achieved while flying the Bf 109, as were his 14 victories in Spain. In December 1941, JG 51 was officially bestowed the name 'Mölders' in honour of its star pilot.

In the fraternity of the Luftwaffe's *Jagdflieger*, many of the leading pilots knew each other and often worked together in higher command activities. One of Mölders' colleagues in this respect was the iconic Adolf Galland. In the same way that Mölders was a great tactician, exceptional pilot and a user of the Bf 109 to its best advantage, so Galland was an equally gifted pilot who flew the Bf 109 to the best of its performance capabilities and similarly achieved an impressive number of aerial victories.

Ironically, Galland did not begin his combat career as a fighter pilot, and at one time was almost prevented from flying altogether. Born on 19 March 1912 in Westerholt (a village now a part of present-day Herten), Galland began his aeronautical activities by learning to fly gliders – an established way for aspiring pilots to take to the air in Germany because flying activity in powered aircraft had been restricted by the Treaty of Versailles following World War I. He subsequently gained his pilot's licence for powered aircraft at the *Deutsche Verkehrsfliegerschule* (German Commercial Flying School) in Braunschweig during 1932.

For a short time Galland flew commercial aircraft for the airline Deutsche Luft Hansa (as it was then known), but he was also courted by the military. He eventually joined the Luftwaffe in 1935, but suffered a crash later that year in a Fw 44 biplane trainer which left him with injuries that threatened his flying career. In particular, he had an eye problem as a result of the accident. However, using means that have sometimes been described as 'mischievous', Galland was able to return to flying. But a second crash, this time in an Ar 68E fighter, resulted in questions being asked of his flying abilities. Again, he was able to evade being grounded.

The onset of the Spanish Civil War gave Galland a chance to prove himself in an operational environment, and he was one of the early volunteers who joined Germany's *Legion Condor* to fly for the Spanish Nationalist forces of Gen Franco. In Spain he was posted to He 51B-equipped 3.J/88, which was increasingly tasked with undertaking ground-attack missions. Galland flew his first combat sortie on 24 July 1937, and eventually became the commanding officer of 3.J/88. While with this unit he developed tactics for air-ground missions that would later prove influential in the development of close air support doctrines for the wartime Luftwaffe.

Galland relinquished command of 3.J/88 near the end of May 1938 and was replaced by Mölders. Before leaving Spain, however, he had the chance to fly the Bf 109, which would soon replace the He 51Bs of 3.J/88. He was immediately impressed by the Messerschmitt fighter.

On his return to Germany, Galland was involved in developing the tactics for air-ground operations, and he tested various new types including the Henschel Hs 129 ground-attack design. For the Polish campaign, he was somewhat irritated to be assigned to Hs 123-equipped II.(Schl)/LG 2, which specialised in ground-attack operations. Galland had hoped to be posted to a fighter unit so that he could fly the Bf 109 in combat. His only consolation was his promotion to Hauptmann.

Galland's chance to become a Bf 109 pilot in the frontline only came about because he was able to convince medical personnel that flying in open-cockpit biplanes (of which the Hs 123 was one) was detrimental to his health, and the cause of the rheumatism that he suffered from. This ruse worked, and in February 1940 he was assigned to the *Stab* of Oberstleutnant Max Ibel's JG 27. This *Geschwader* was comparatively new, having only been created on 1 October 1939.

A Bf 109E of 1./JG 1 has its engine fettled behind a gaggle of Hs 123s at an austere airfield somewhere in France in the spring of 1940. The rugged ground-attack aircraft belonged to II.(Schl)/LG 2, which was the unit Hauptmann Adolf Galland had served with during the Poland campaign. (Tony Holmes Collection)

Galland's elation at finally being assigned to a Bf 109E-equipped fighter unit was tempered by the fact that he was officially the unit's Adjutant, which was in theory a non-combat desk job. However, being proficient at preventing such minor inconveniences from getting in his way, Galland soon teamed up with his old colleague from *Legion Condor* days, Hauptmann Werner Mölders. By then, the ranking German ace of the Spanish Civil War was *Gruppenkommandeur* of III./JG 53, and he tutored Galland in many of the tactical lessons he had been developing since his time in Spain.

During that period, Mölders' tactical thinking had been having a major influence on Luftwaffe doctrine, and the opportunity for Galland to put these ideas into practice came a little later in the *Blitzkrieg* era. On 10 May 1940, when German forces invaded the Low Countries and France, JG 27 was involved right at the start of hostilities by supporting the assault on Belgium. Galland was by then able to fly in combat, and had as his wingman Leutnant Gustav Rödel also from *Stab* JG 27.

On the third day of the offensive (12 May), west of the Belgian town of Liège, Galland achieved the first aerial victories of his illustrious combat career. Together with his JG 27 colleagues, he bounced a formation of RAF Hurricanes from No 87 Sqn that were flying top cover for Blenheim light bombers. The Blenheims were trying to stop the German advance by attacking key bridges, but JG 27 easily broke up the Hurricane escort, which scattered in all directions with no apparent discipline or tactical know-how.

Galland shot down two of the RAF fighters for his first aerial victories. In so doing, he and Rödel followed Mölders' dogfighting tactics to the letter,

---

0915 hrs, 12 MAY 1940

WEST OF LIÈGE

1 Hauptmann Adolf Galland and his wingman Leutnant Gustav Rödel, both from *Stab* JG 27, spot a formation of RAF Blenheim IVs being escorted by Hurricane Is of No 87 Sqn.

2 The *Jagdwaffe* pilots position themselves in the classic 'up sun' location, making them difficult to see from below. Then, keeping their *Rotte* formation, they dive onto the top Hurricanes, hitting Sgt Frank 'Dinky' Howell's aircraft in a classic surprise attack.

3 Badly hit, and left alone by his scattering squadronmates, Howell tries to evade but is struck again as Galland presses home his attack for a second time. Howell's rudder is shot away.

4 Out of control, Howell's Hurricane plunges towards the ground, breaking up as it falls to earth. Howell successfully bails out and lives to tell the tale.

5 Moments later, Flg Off Jack Campbell comes under attack by Galland, and the Canadian pilot wings over to evade his pursuers before diving into a gap in the clouds hoping to shake off the Messerschmitts.

6 However, Galland is able to stay with Campbell, emerging at low-level and riddling the fleeing Hurricane with cannon fire.

7 Mortally hit, the Hurricane zooms upwards, stalls, then crashes into the ground, killing Campbell.

FOLLOWING PAGES

their initial surprise attack using superior height and subsequent follow-up to make a second deadly firing opportunity, gaining complete success. The first Hurricane that fell to Galland's machine gun and cannon armament was L1632, flown by Sgt Frank Howell, who escaped by parachute. The No 87 Sqn pilot later recalled, 'They came from the sun with altitude advantage and I never saw them. Suddenly there was a shattering noise and the cockpit was full of burnt cordite.' Galland followed this up moments later by downing L1970, flown by Canadian Flg Off Jack Campbell, who was killed in the attack.

Galland claimed a third Hurricane later that same day. He assumed that his opponents were Belgian-operated, partly due to the out-dated two-bladed Watts propellers of at least some of the machines that he was encountering. But the Belgian Hurricanes even by that date had been either destroyed on their airfields or rendered inoperative by the German advance on the ground.

Of the incident, Galland later wrote in his autobiography *The First and the Last*:

> Some five miles west of Liège, my flight companion and I dove from an altitude of about 12,000ft on a flight of eight Hurricanes flying 3,000ft below us. I had one of the eight in my gunsight. I closed in more and more without being noticed. I gave him my first burst from a distance which, considering the situation, was still too great. I was dead on the target. The poor devil at last noticed what it was all about. He took rather clumsy avoiding action which brought him into the fire of my companion.
>
> The other seven Hurricanes made no effort to come to the aid of their comrade in distress, but made off in all directions. After a second attack my opponent spun down in spirals minus his rudder. Parts of the wings came off. Another burst would have been a waste of ammunition. I immediately went after another of the scattered Hurricanes. This one tried to escape by diving, but I was soon on her tail at a distance of 100 yards. The Belgian did a half-roll and disappeared through a hole in the clouds. I did not lose track of him, and attacked again from very close quarters. The aeroplane zoomed for a second, stalled, and dove vertically to the ground from a height of only 1,500ft. During a patrol flight that afternoon, I shot down my third opponent out of a formation of five Hurricanes near Tirlemont [Tienen].

Galland was fully aware that his Bf 109 had a superior rate of climb and was faster in a dive than the Hurricane, but that the latter was more manoeuvrable. 'Emil' pilots were advised to avoid close-in dogfighting with the Hurricane and employ the 'bounce' manoeuvre instead – a tactic much favoured by Werner Mölders and used so successfully on this occasion by Galland.

Post-war, Galland recalled this action on 12 May 1940 when interviewed by the RAF's Air Historical Branch, pointing out that:

> The Belgians for the most part flew antiquated Hurricanes which were out-of-date, in which even more experienced pilots could have done little against our new 109E. Their performance was far inferior to that of the Messerschmitt fighter as regards both maximum speed in level flight and rate of climb. The modern Spitfires were slower than our aeroplanes by about 10–15mph but they could perform steeper and tighter turns.

German ammunition and armament were manifestly better than those of the British. But even more important than these technical drawbacks were the outmoded tactics used by the British fighters. Generally speaking, they flew in close formation of squadron strength in order to peel off immediately before making an attack. German fighters, on the other hand, flew in wide, open formations – a tactic evolved during the Spanish Civil War.

Galland was awarded the Iron Cross First Class on 22 May, by which time he had lodged claims for seven Allied aircraft, all achieved while flying with the *Stab* of JG 27 in the Bf 109E-3.

Like other *Jagdwaffe* units, JG 27 moved forward into captured territory to follow the fighting as May wore on, using permanent airfields or improvised airstrips that had been overrun by the rapidly advancing Wehrmacht. However, it was during the at times furious aerial battles over Dunkirk in late May that Galland first encountered RAF Spitfires in any numbers. These he immediately realised were the main foes of the *Jagdwaffe* and its Messerschmitts. He later explained, 'My first serious encounters with the RAF took place during the battle of Dunkirk. The RAF made a great and successful effort to provide air cover for the remarkable evacuation operation.' Nevertheless, the Germans emerged victorious from the Dunkirk fighting, despite the large numbers of British and French troops that were evacuated.

It was during this period that Galland faced a new challenge. By then an established fighter leader, he was elevated to command III./JG 26 on 6 June. Eighteen days later, an old colleague of his from the *Legion Condor* days, Major Gotthard Handrick, took overall command of the *Geschwader*.

Galland ended the *Blitzkrieg* period with 13 confirmed aerial victories. After a short lull in activity following the defeat of France, during the subsequent months JG 26 was embroiled in fighting on the Channel Front, with the unit fully involved in many of the major air battles of the Battle of Britain. On 18 July (according to his memoirs) Galland was promoted to Major, and was awarded the Knight's Cross of the Iron Cross on the 29th of that month.

In a major career move, Galland was elevated to the overall command of JG 26 on 22 August when Göring dismissed Handrick. With the course of the Battle of Britain progressing increasingly badly for the *Jagdwaffe*, several unit commanders were removed from their posts by an increasingly belligerent Göring, who had made extravagant claims about the Luftwaffe's expected easy victory over the RAF.

Galland went on to enjoy a glittering career in the Luftwaffe, reaching high command and progressing up through the ranks. In November 1941 he replaced Oberst Werner Mölders as *Inspekteur der Jagdflieger* following the

Despite having started the Battle of France without a victory to his name, and after spending the early months of World War II flying Hs 123 ground-attack aircraft, Hauptmann Adolf Galland soon proved his abilities as a fighter pilot with *Stab* JG 27 by claiming 13 victories in five weeks. Seen here in a typically relaxed pose, with a cigar in his left hand, Galland is wearing an RAF Bomber Command issue Irvin sheepskin flying suit over his service dress. Although very bulky for the Bf 109's narrow, cramped cockpit, such suits were highly coveted amongst *Jagdflieger* during the winter months on the Channel Front. (EN Archive)

former's tragic death in the accident while travelling to attend the funeral of Generaloberst Udet. Galland had been flying regularly in combat up to that time on the Channel Front, and he disliked the idea of being taken out of the frontline. He subsequently presided over increasingly difficult times for the *Jagdflieger*, as the tide of the war turned against the Germans and the arrival of the US Army Air Forces (USAAF) in the skies of northwestern Europe gradually overwhelmed the Luftwaffe.

Galland was relieved of his command in January 1945, having completely fallen out of favour with Göring. The following month, however, he was put in charge of a new unit, *Jagdverband* 44, equipped with Messerschmitt Me 262A jet fighters. Galland finished the war with up to 104 aerial victories (some sources quote 102 or 100), all achieved in the west, and the vast majority of them while flying various marks of Bf 109. Clearly the lessons that he had learned from Werner Mölders on tactics and flying the Bf 109 in combat had stood him in good stead.

Galland passed away on 9 February 1996 at Oberwinter in Rhineland-Palatinate, having become one of the last surviving exponents of the Bf 109.

CHAPTER 4
WEAPON OF WAR

When it was designed in the mid-1930s, the Bf 109 was one of the most advanced warplanes of its day. Willy Messerschmitt and his team of engineers embraced many of the new concepts that were coming to the fore in fighter design for their new aircraft. These included the low-wing cantilever monoplane layout, all-metal structure and the use of a modern, high-performance (for its day) inline piston engine. The whole design of the Bf 109 was clean and well thought out. It was a world away from the externally rigged, canvas-covered biplane fighters that many nations were at that time still using as frontline equipment.

The Bf 109 dated from a specification released as far back as 1933 when the Nazis successfully gained power in Germany, and at once set about modernising and massively expanding the nation's armed forces. The new RLM issued a far-reaching requirement in July 1933 calling for an innovative and advanced single-seat fighter, with a number of specific qualities. In addition to the normal prerequisites for a fighter of its day, one quirk was the need for the planned aircraft to be transportable by rail. No mention was made of wing armament or of long range/endurance.

These realities were of great importance in determining the size, design and armament layout of the new fighter. The Bf 109 arose out of these diverse requirements and, in particular, the type's narrow-track main undercarriage, which caused so many problems to its pilots on take-off and landing from the start, was a result of the need for the aircraft to be rail transportable. As designed and manufactured, the Bf 109's undercarriage was attached to the fuselage, allowing the wings to be easily removed while the fuselage stood on its undercarriage, causing the latter's track to be extremely narrow. Landing in a crosswind onto a paved surface would prove to be a challenge even for a seasoned pilot. Many novice aviators were caught out by this undercarriage arrangement, leading to ground loops and inevitable damage to the airframe that was often terminal.

Four manufacturers responded with prototypes to the July 1933 requirement. The design from Willy Messerschmitt and his colleagues at the Bayerische Flugzeugwerke AG was eventually victorious, although one of its rivals, the Heinkel He 112, was a good contender that was also eventually series produced,

The initial production version of the Bf 109 was the Jumo 210D-powered B-model, whose simple armament comprised two 7.92mm MG 17 machine guns in the upper forward fuselage ahead of the cockpit. It was this type that entered service during the first half of 1937, and saw action in the Spanish Civil War with the *Legion Condor*. A small number were still on the books of several *Jagdwaffe* units in 1939, but by then they had been largely replaced by the Bf 109D, which was itself in the process of being phased out in favour of the DB 601A-powered Bf 109E-1. (Author's Collection)

mainly for export. That Messerschmitt succeeded at all was a breakthrough because some in the Third Reich's hierarchy had a profound dislike for him and his designs.

Following its successful first flight in late May 1935, the Bf 109 showed great promise. Series manufacture was initiated in the autumn of 1936, with the first production aircraft entering service in February 1937 with II./JG 132. The Bf 109 went from strength to strength, and proved at once to be a war-winner – the contribution of the early Bf 109s that were sent to Spain and flown by German pilots of the *Legion Condor* in support of Gen Franco's rebel forces helped towards the Spanish Nationalist success of 1939, which was the first major fascist victory in warfare.

The initial austere but nonetheless capable Junkers Jumo-powered Bf 109 versions gave way on the production lines during 1938 to the Daimler-Benz-powered Bf 109E, which was the major fighter type equipping most of the *Jagdwaffe's* operational units when they supported the invasion of Poland in September 1939 in the opening days of what became World War II. The contribution made by the Bf 109 to Germany's success during the first months of the conflict cannot be overestimated. It eventually fought on all fronts for the Luftwaffe, and in the early days the Bf 109 was tremendously successful, being a quantum leap ahead of most fighter opponents it faced in the opening months of that war.

In terms of manufacture, the Bf 109B was the first major production series. Armed with just two 7.92mm MG 17 machine guns, the fighter was powered by the carburettor-equipped 680hp (this and all other horsepower ratings in this chapter refer to take-off power, and are the English-language equivalents of German horsepower, which is slightly different to British parameters) Jumo 210D engine. Early Bf 109Bs were fitted with a wooden Schwarz two-bladed fixed-pitch propeller, but later production examples had VDM two-bladed variable-pitch propeller units – there was no differentiation by Bf 109B sub-type in Messerschmitt documents to tell between them. The B-model saw early action

The Junkers Jumo 210 inline engine powered all the early Bf 109 marks up to and including the Bf 109D. The B- and D-models featured the Jumo 210D with a normal carburettor, while the small number of Bf 109Cs manufactured were fitted with the fuel-injected Jumo 210G. The left-hand 7.92mm MG 17 machine gun can be clearly seen in this image, mounted in the upper forward fuselage. (Author's Collection)

in Spain during the first half of 1937. It is confirmed that 344 were built.

The Bf 109C was similar to the basic B-model, but with various detail improvements and an increase in internal fuel, as well as the addition of wing-mounted MG 17s (one in each wing in the C-1 version) which the Bf 109 had not originally been designed to carry. The Jumo 210G fuel-injection engine was fitted, this powerplant producing 700hp for take-off. Only 58 Bf 109Cs were built.

The final Jumo-powered variant was the Bf 109D, or 'Dora', fitted with the carburettor-equipped Jumo 210D engine. This was a comparatively simple supercharged engine of relatively low power output (660hp) that used B4 fuel (87 octane). The 'Dora' included the detail improvements of the Bf 109C and featured the four MG 17 armament of the Bf 109C-1. No fewer than 657 examples of these somewhat austere, but nevertheless capable, fighters were built. Due their availability in significant numbers, Bf 109Ds played a larger part in the Polish campaign during September 1939 than they are often given credit for.

With an early He 111 in the background, a Jumo-engined Bf 109D-1 shows off its upper forward fuselage armament of two 7.92mm MG 17 machine guns. The early style, rounded-top cockpit canopy of the Jumo-engined Bf 109s seen here was replaced during 'Emil' manufacture by the more angular flat-topped canopy that eventually contained head armour for the pilot. (Author's Collection)

The Bf 109E, or 'Emil', was the first version of the Messerschmitt to be truly combat-ready to take on high-performance fighters such as the Spitfire and D.520. It represented a major step forward in Bf 109 design, being fitted with Daimler-Benz's outstanding supercharged and fuel-injected DB 601-series engine. There had previously been several one-off prototype/development airframes that had been powered by the initial DB 600, and they have since mistakenly been identified as Bf 109D production aircraft. However, in reality, no production D-models were fitted with Daimler-Benz engines, and it was the Bf 109E that introduced the DB 600-series to frontline service.

To install the DB 601 powerplant, the entire forward fuselage was re-designed, the supercharger air intake relocated from the upper right-hand cowling of the Jumo-powered Bf 109 to a new mid position on the left-hand side of the engine cowling, and many detail changes made to auxiliary equipment. The large lower nose radiator for engine coolant of the Jumo-engined version was moved to a

A Bf 109E displaying the Daimler-Benz DB 601A engine that was introduced with the 'Emil'. A much bulkier unit than the Jumo 210 fitted to the Bf 109B to D fighters, the DB 601-series was more powerful than the Junkers engine and gave the Bf 109 greater performance. The 'Emil' retained the same upper forward fuselage armament as the Jumo-powered models of two 7.92mm MG 17 machine guns. (Author's Collection)

new underwing position, its place then being taken by a shallower oil radiator.

The DB 601's fuel-injection was markedly different to the early models of Rolls-Royce Merlin engine that powered initial production versions of the Hurricane and Spitfire, which relied on a carburettor and were prone to cut out if the aircraft was flown inverted for more than a short time. This was clearly a disadvantage for the British machines in dogfighting, especially when flying against a Bf 109E. The DB 601A of 1,100hp was used by most Bf 109Es, this engine having been introduced into series manufacture from November 1937. A three-bladed VDM variable-pitch metal propeller unit was standard for the Bf 109E – most previous models had relied on a two-bladed variable-pitch propeller.

There were many sub-variants during the Bf 109E's production, which started, appropriately, with the E-1. During the E-3 series, a new, square-framed cockpit canopy was introduced that replaced the more rounded shape of previous versions, although some older aircraft had this new canopy retrofitted. Factory-installed armour plate within the canopy for the pilot's head was included from the E-4 onwards. The Bf 109E was very widely manufactured, and was produced from the second half of 1938 onwards, entering increasingly numerous Luftwaffe service during the first half of 1939.

The 'Emil' was a well-armed warplane, reflecting the evolving German military thinking of the World War II era in terms of fighter aircraft armament. The Luftwaffe was convinced that heavy-calibre weapons in comparatively small numbers were preferable to the British concept of the late 1930s that made use of up to eight rapidly firing rifle-calibre machine guns. The RAF eventually modified this concept to also include heavier-calibre weapons, while the Bf 109 was developed in time into a formidable fighter and, later, a ground-attack aircraft – although the addition of some weapon systems to its comparatively small and compact airframe adversely affected performance. Indeed, throughout its service life the Bf 109 underwent considerable up-gunning and weapons evolution specifically to suit operational requirements.

One of the personalities who influenced Luftwaffe thinking regarding warplane armament was the famous fighter ace Adolf Galland. During the early 1930s, when he was flying for Deutsche Luft Hansa, Galland was courted to join the newly forming Luftwaffe. In the summer of 1933 he travelled to Italy and underwent some training with its air force, the *Regia Aeronautica*. Galland was interested by the Italian preference for heavier-calibre weapons in fighter aircraft, and it was possible that this influenced his thinking into the employment of a combination of machine guns and cannon for fighters. In later years, particularly during the *Blitzkrieg* era in the early months of World War II, this proved to be a winning combination of weapons in the Bf 109.

As previously noted, the original armament of the initial B-model production aircraft comprised two 7.92mm Rheinmetall-Borsig MG 17 machine guns, mounted in the upper forward fuselage ahead of the cockpit and synchronised to fire through the propeller arc. Because of the arrangement of the magazines/ammunition chutes, the left-hand weapon was set slightly further forward than that on the right. There had been the intention to install a third MG 17 centrally in the engine compartment to fire through the propeller hub (the so-called 'engine-mounted' installation), but this was found to be impracticable even though the Jumo 210 engine could be configured to allow this. Each gun had 500 rounds, but in later models this was doubled to 1,000 rounds.

In the Bf 109C the armament was uprated, partly as a result of operational experience with the B-model during the Spanish Civil War, to include a further MG 17 in each wing outboard of the propeller arc and, therefore, not needing to be synchronised. This was additional to the established two MG 17s in the upper forward fuselage. The wing guns had 420 rounds each (some factory documentation suggests this was increased to 500 rounds). It was intended that a centrally mounted, Oerlikon licence-built MG FF 20mm cannon would be fitted, but again attempts to perfect this 'engine-mounted' installation were not successful due to vibration and other issues. This armament arrangement stayed the same for the Bf 109D, the last of the Jumo-engined variants.

The MG 17 was an air-cooled machine gun with electric firing, and pneumatic charging – the compressed air bottles for which were located in the fuselage, although on some later models of the Bf 109 these were moved to the wings. The MG 17 had a rate of fire, in its best optimum operating conditions, of 1,200 rounds per minute, although as with most airborne weapons at that time the operating altitude, outside temperature and other related features could significantly reduce that figure.

This basic weapons configuration of two upper forward fuselage and two wing-mounted MG 17s was carried on into the first Daimler-Benz-powered production variant of the 'Emil', the E-1. This was the initial major production model of the Bf 109E-series, and was a significant part of the Luftwaffe's inventory during 1939 and in the early months of World War II.

However, the next major production model, the E-3, introduced a much heavier armament. Although the two MG 17 machine guns in the upper forward fuselage were retained for the E-3, the wing-mounted MG 17s were replaced by an MG FF 20mm cannon, one in each wing. The latter was a much larger and heavier weapon than the MG 17, and it was mounted slightly further outboard – a prominent bulge on the underside of the wing was introduced so that the cannon, and its associated 60-round drum magazine, could be accommodated within the 'Emil's' slim wing structure.

Overall, the Bf 109 had not been intended to house such a bulky weapon within its mainplanes. Indeed, the Bf 109's wing had not originally been

Mounted in the upper forward fuselage above the engine, the two 7.92mm MG 17 machine guns of the Jumo-engined Bf 109s and the 'Emil' were staggered as seen here, with the left-hand weapon being slightly further forward. This Bf 109E-1 belonged to JG 26, and it had the luxury of being worked on inside a hangar. During the Battle of France in particular, such niceties were left far behind, as fighter units followed the frontline and were often based in austere surroundings. (Author's Collection)

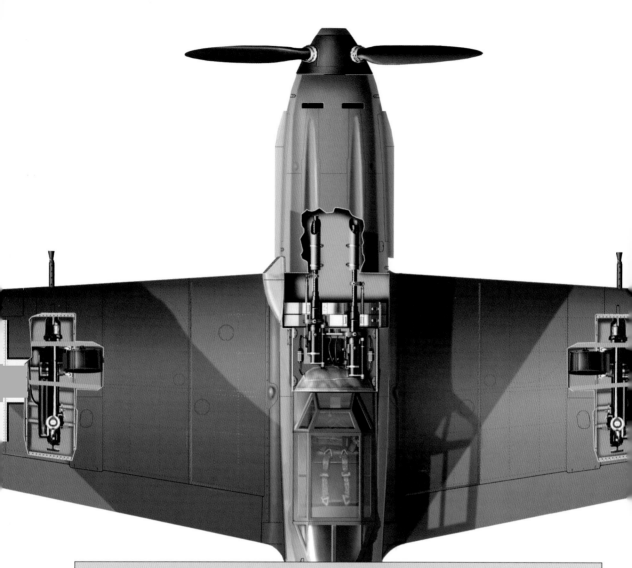

Bf 109E-3 ARMAMENT

Like previous Jumo-engined variants of the Bf 109, the Bf 109E was fitted with a pair of Rheinmetall MG 17 7.92mm machine guns in the upper forward fuselage ahead of the cockpit. Each weapon had a magazine holding 1,000 rounds per gun. Note how the guns are staggered, with the port MG 17 being set slightly forward by the width of the ammunition feed chute. The Bf 109E-3 differed from the previous E-1 and E-2 models of the 'Emil' by having the single MG 17 in each wing replaced by a licence-built Oerlikon MG FF 20mm cannon. The barrel of this weapon protruded beyond the wing leading edge, and it was a major distinguishing point for the Bf 109E-3 and subsequent versions of the 'Emil'. A fairing was needed beneath the wing of cannon-armed Bf 109s to accommodate part of the 60-round drum of 20mm cannon shells.

designed with the carriage of weapons, internal or external, as a primary consideration at all.

At that time the MG FF was already becoming obsolete, and it had a slow rate of fire of some 530 rounds per minute. The weapon did, however, represent

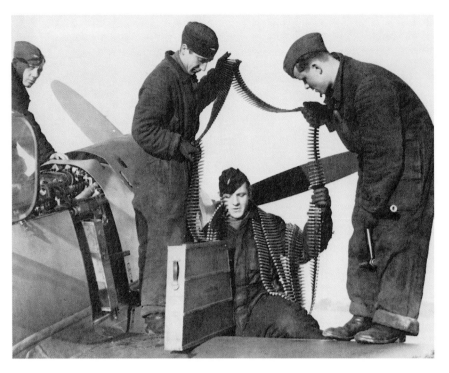

A team of armourers in the Luftwaffe's distinctive dark-coloured overalls load ammunition boxes for the upper forward fuselage-mounted MG 17 machine guns fitted to an early build Bf 109E-1. Each gun had sufficient ammunition storage for 1,000 rounds. Note that the groundcrew have removed an area of the cowling immediately forward of the cockpit so as to gain easy access to the guns and their ammunition boxes. (EN Archive)

The Bf 109E-3 boasted a heavier punch than previous variants of the Messerschmitt fighter thanks to the replacement of its twin MG 17 machine guns with two MG FF 20mm cannon. Larger and heavier weapons than the 7.92mm machine guns, the MG FFs were mounted further outboard. They also required a prominent bulge on the underside of each wing to accommodate a single 60-round drum magazine. Here, an armourer is installing a magazine for the cannon housed in the starboard wing. (EN Archive)

a significant up-gunning of the Bf 109. It was also fitted in the wing of the Bf 109E-4 and the later E-7 version, in a configuration identical to the E-3. There is also documented and photographic evidence that some Bf 109Cs (as the Bf 109C-3) and E-1s similarly had this wing cannon arrangement presumably as a result of upgrade work.

An attempt was additionally made to centrally locate the MG FF in the so-called 'engine-mounted' position for the 'Emil' series, and the rare Bf 109E-2 and some E-3s have been claimed to have had this configuration. If that was the case it would only have been in limited numbers, and there is no evidence that this particular layout was ever used in combat by early 'Emils'.

Although the MG FF considerably up-gunned the Bf 109E-3, some Luftwaffe pilots were not entirely impressed. Oberleutnant Hans Schmoller-Haldy of I./JG 54 pointed out:

I thought the Spitfire was better armed than the '109. The cannon fitted to the 'Emil' were not much use against enemy fighters, and the machine guns on top of the engine often suffered stoppages. The cannon were good if they scored a hit, but their rate of fire was low. The cannon had greater range than the machine guns, but we were always told that in a dogfight one could not hope to hit anything at ranges greater than 50m.

An image from the official handbook for the Bf 109B, showing the *Revi* C/12C reflector gunsight. It was used throughout most of the Jumo-engined Bf 109 production (except for some very early examples of the B-model), and continued during Bf 109E manufacture. The unit was installed offset slightly to the right on the upper part of the instrument panel. Note the handholds within the canopy frame to aid the pilot when entering and exiting the aircraft. (Author's Collection)

A development of the MG FF, the MG FF/M which fired slightly different types of cannon shells was made available for use in the Bf 109 and was fitted instead of the standard MG FF in later aircraft, notably many of the Bf 109E-4 version and subsequent marks of the 'Emil'.

For the purpose of weapons aiming, Bf 109 pilots were provided with a reflector gunsight. This type of equipment was known to the Germans as a *Reflexvisier* (often shortened to *Revi*). In the initial production Bf 109B, the model installed was a rudimentary *Revi* 3-series unit, and this was also fitted to some examples of the later Jumo 210-engined Bf 109s and early 'Emils'.

The most developed version in the *Revi* 3-series was the *Revi* 3C. However, it was superseded during Bf 109E production by the excellent and very simple to operate *Revi* C/12-series. These gunsights had no computing capacity, but were much preferred by Luftwaffe pilots to the original *Revi* 3-series units. However, some Bf 109s nevertheless retained a rudimentary ring and bead type sight in addition to the gunsight. The *Revi* C/12 came in two basic versions, the *Revi* C/12C for simple gun/cannon sighting in aerial combat and the *Revi* C/12D for multiple weapon use, including bomb-aiming for fighter-bomber operations. Whatever mark of *Revi* gunsight, the unit was mounted slightly offset to the right in front of the pilot on a bracket protruding from the upper edge of the instrument panel.

The Bf 109 thus went to war in September 1939 as a well-armed and capable fighter, already thoroughly combat-tested in Spanish skies. But with the addition of the MG FF 20mm cannon in the wings from the Bf 109E-3 onwards, it became an even more formidable opponent.

CHAPTER 5

ART OF WAR

When the Bf 109B entered service in February 1937, the first Luftwaffe units to receive the new fighter were I. and II./JG 132 'Richthofen'. These *Gruppen* were therefore at the forefront of formulating tactics for the combat use of the type. With their existing equipment primarily consisting of the obsolescent He 51B, the 'Richthofen' pilots were keen to learn about their new high-performance warplane.

But this euphoria was short-lived with the coming of a complete change of direction. The first Bf 109s to see frontline action were the Messerschmitts of various marks that were sent to Spain and duly operated with Germany's *Legion Condor*. Spain was the proving ground for the Bf 109, and lessons learned there were to influence the future design and direction of the type's development. And in a related but different way, knowledge gained in the war-torn skies over Spain also had a profound influence on the Luftwaffe's overall tactical thinking.

Initial combat for the *Legion Condor* had involved biplane fighters, of which the He 51B was the most effective. However, the arrival of the first Bf 109Bs from Germany during March 1937 began a major change in operational capability. The Luftwaffe rushed initial examples of the Bf 109, and its contemporary the He 112, to Spain to aid Gen Franco's Nationalist forces, partly in response to the supply by the Soviet Union to the legitimate Spanish government of a growing number of modern warplanes and other military equipment.

The potentially most deadly of the new aircraft types supplied to the Republicans was the diminutive monoplane I-16, which was more than a match for the increasingly obsolete He 51B. Also arriving in Spain from the Soviet Union was the twin-engined SB-2 monoplane bomber, which was faster in a straight line than the He 51B.

In a sense, the Bf 109B was thrown in at the deep end in Spain. Tactics for such a fast and manoeuvrable warplane had not been thought out, and the Spanish Civil War was effectively the first time that a modern fighter had entered combat in any numbers against a potentially equal foe.

By 1937, only a small number of air forces had started to introduce modern monoplane fighters into their inventories. Even those that had instituted a modernisation programme were still stuck in the tactical mind-set of the past decade or so. Some viewed the ability to perform strict formation flying as a vitally important trait for frontline fighter pilots. A number of air forces, the RAF included, thrilled crowds at the equivalents of today's airshows with demonstrations of precision flying using comparatively slow but very manoeuvrable biplanes. Indeed, a crowd pleaser at the annual RAF Display at Hendon in the 1930s was close formation flying by several biplanes loosely linked together with rubber cables.

That sort of precise flying was fine for the era of frontline biplanes with no one to fight in aerial combat, but it had clearly become absolutely outdated overnight with the arrival in service of high-performance, fast monoplane fighters like the Bf 109. Nevertheless, the response of most air forces, the Luftwaffe included, was to continue with the established neat and well-drilled 'parade ground' formation flying, even with the introduction of the new monoplane fighters. In particular, the long-established concept of the rigid three-aeroplane 'vic' formation (*Kette* in German) persisted long after it had become obsolete.

There was also a similarly out-dated 'vic' formation of five aircraft (a tight group of fighters forming the letter 'V', pointing in the direction of their forward flight), which was a feature of post-World War I thinking and could be found in RAF training manuals of that era.

Events in Spain completely changed this outlook. It soon became obvious that the rigid three-aeroplane 'vic' was of little use for attack or mutual protection. Only the tail of the leading aircraft of the 'vic' could be adequately covered, leaving the two outer aircraft vulnerable to interception from behind by opposing fighters. In any case it was too rigid a system to take into combat, giving an easy target for opposing fighters to aim at and even allowing aiming to be made easier for defensive gunners in bombers.

Pilots from JG 132 'Richthofen' demonstrate their expertise at precision flying by forming up into three tightly flown *Ketten* high above Cologne during the mid-1930s. The unmistakable twin spires of the city's great Gothic cathedral and the River Rhine beyond can just be seen emerging from the early morning mist. (Tony Holmes Collection)

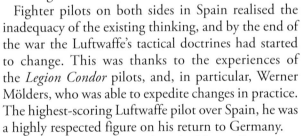
Fighter pilots on both sides in Spain realised the inadequacy of the existing thinking, and by the end of the war the Luftwaffe's tactical doctrines had started to change. This was thanks to the experiences of the *Legion Condor* pilots, and, in particular, Werner Mölders, who was able to expedite changes in practice. The highest-scoring Luftwaffe pilot over Spain, he was a highly respected figure on his return to Germany.

Mölders had determined, as had his colleagues in J/88, that a battle formation based on two rather than three or five aircraft should form the basis of air combat tactics for fighter pilots. Eventually a completely new system was devised, based on two- and four-aircraft groups.

In German parlance, the basic two-element formation or pair came to be called a *Rotte*, and consisted of a leader (*Rottenführer*) and his wingman (*Rottenflieger*, sometimes known by the nickname *Katschmarek*). The leader was the primary member of the pairing in having the first choice for attacking an enemy aircraft, with his wingman covering his tail (and the wingman's own tail too), thus freeing up the leader to concentrate on shooting down the opponent. It was up to the wingman to keep up with his leader, no matter what manoeuvres were needed in the dogfight that they were involved in. In level flight, the two aircraft would normally fly up to approximately 200m apart, with the leader slightly ahead.

This basic formation was further developed by Mölders and his colleagues into a four-aeroplane *Schwarm*. It was found that a loose four-aircraft formation, roughly in line abreast but not rigidly so, provided an improved all-round field of vision while giving excellent mutual defence, and allowed each pilot to be on the look-out for potential enemies. It permitted greater combat flexibility and also encouraged individual pilot initiative and versatility. The free-ranging formation could easily be broken down into two *Rotten* depending on the particular combat situation that the pilots found themselves in.

Although a wartime propaganda photograph, this image nevertheless is historically interesting in showing a *Kette* of three Bf 109Es in the type of three-aircraft battle formation that was superseded by the *Rotte* and the larger *Schwarm* ('finger-four') formation. These Messerschmitts were from JG 77 according to the original caption that accompanied the photograph. (Author's Collection)

Some of the fighter leaders preferred the *Schwarm* to fly with one *Rotte* to one side and slightly ahead of the other, but there were no fixed rules on this, and in practice the pilots got to know each others' preferences and worked together effectively within the basic system.

Normally three of the *Schwarm* formations would make up a *Staffel*. If they flew together in formation, which was not by any means always the case, the three *Schwarm* formations would fly in such a way that they were stepped up in line astern, occasionally but more rarely in echelon.

This basic formation was also eventually adopted by other air forces, and is well known in the RAF as the 'finger-four' with the participants spaced out corresponding to the fingertips of an outstretched hand.

Mölders' tour of duty in Spain ended in December 1938 and he returned to Germany, where he was soon in a position from which he could positively influence Luftwaffe tactical policy. Delegated to his staff position in the department of the *Inspekteur der Jagdflieger* in Berlin, he was one of several experienced officers who duly set about devising new fighter pilot tactics derived from experience of the air war in Spain and based on the high performance of the Bf 109. By that time the Bf 109 had become the Luftwaffe's premier (and only) frontline day fighter, and it was at the heart of this complete review and development of tactics.

Mölders is often credited with inventing or at the very least modifying a manoeuvre called the 'cross-over turn'. This tactic was already known, and had even been in use by the RAF with a five-aircraft formation. However, it had commonly been employed with a very close spacing between each aircraft (sometimes as little as 30m), which was dangerous. The German adaptation, as pioneered in Spain, used just the four aircraft of the *Schwarm*, with a much wider separation between each aircraft and each *Rotte* (of at least 200m) to avoid the possibility of a collision between the participating fighters when performing this manoeuvre.

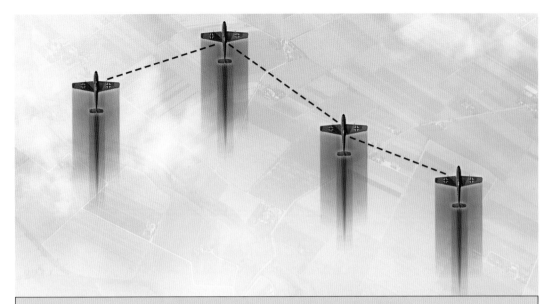

FOUR-AIRCRAFT *SCHWARM* FORMATION

Derived from combat experience and developed principally by Werner Mölders, battle formations employed by Bf 109D/E units during the early months of World War II centred on the two-aircraft *Rotte* and the four aircraft *Schwarm*, the latter containing two of the former. The *Schwarm* was led by a *Rottenführer*, whose position was monitored and guarded by his wingman. The two *Rotten* flew in a loose line abreast formation, but with the rear *Rotte* echeloned back so that effectively the wingman concept extended by *Rotte* to the whole *Schwarm*. Generally, it was found that the best distance between aircraft was around 180–200m.

The basic *Schwarm* doctrine was a revelation, being a loose four-aircraft pattern in which each pilot could keep watch on his peers in a far more successful way than the rigid strict three-aircraft 'vic' 'textbook' formations flown during the pre-war years. The success of the four-aircraft tactical arrangement during the *Blitzkrieg* period led to other countries adopting it. For the RAF, which used this type of formation from the Battle of Britain onwards, it came to be called the 'finger-four' – although the RAF's interpretation was of a more rigid grouping resembling (from above) the position of the fingertips of a hand's outstretched fingers.

Therefore, by the start of World War II, the Luftwaffe had in place a tactical supremacy for its fighters that stood it in good stead for the coming wartime campaigns. No other country had this advanced thinking on tactics at that time. The Germans had basically torn up the rule book on air warfare for fighter aircraft. Just in the way that *Blitzkrieg* was a new type of waging war on land and in the air, so the world of the fighter pilot in the very specific arena of aerial combat between fighters on opposing sides was also changed forever.

In other ways the Germans possessed an awareness of basic combat necessities that additionally set them apart from many of their future potential enemies. A tactic that is nowadays completely taken for granted because it is so obvious, but which was again comparatively 'new' thinking in the late 1930s, was the concept of attacking the enemy 'out of the sun'.

Height advantage was and still is an obvious factor in air combat. Possessing the 'high ground' and thus being able to control the battle and dive on unsuspecting opponents was already known to be an obvious benefit. But taking this to its logical conclusion, diving on an enemy 'out of the sun' held the clear advantage of surprise by allowing the attacker a high level of concealment because pilots at the lower altitude would be unable to see their opponents when looking upwards due to being 'blinded' by the sun. The element of surprise could often determine success or failure in aerial combat.

Two Bf 109Ds practice dogfighting. The aircraft on the right bears the fuselage code '10+N', indicating that it belonged to one of the nightfighter *Staffeln* that were equipped with 'Doras' as a stop-gap until more suitable radar-equipped aircraft became available. The Bf 109D nightfighter units sometimes operated by day if necessary, and these two 'Doras' display the basic working pairing, or *Rotte*, that formed the nucleus of the *Jagdwaffe*'s tactical formation and fighting arrangement. (Author's Collection)

That the Germans were able to perform this manoeuvre on countless occasions during the *Blitzkrieg* era was thanks to two key factors. One was the awareness of the tactical advantages of holding the 'high ground', but the other was the fact that the Bf 109 was capable of doing this. With their Messerschmitts having a higher operating ceiling and better altitude performance than the Polish, Dutch, British and French fighters that they encountered during the opening nine months or so of the war, *Jagdwaffe* pilots used the Bf 109 to its obvious strengths in order to place them in a winning position prior to engaging their foes.

Although these tactics were basically in place by the commencement of World War II, it was an evolutionary process, and work was being carried out at the flying training schools to indoctrinate new students into the importance of tactical awareness and the skills needed for the type of formation flying demanded of the *Rotte* and *Schwarm* system.

In the pre-war period, and during the war years up to 1942, the Luftwaffe's training system worked well. Pilots who had achieved their basic training and gained their 'wings' had already received some indoctrination into tactical awareness. This, together with their flying skills and gunnery, were further honed when they joined the advanced training schools dedicated to producing proficient fighter pilots for the *Jagdwaffe*. These existed under the title of *Jagdfliegerschulen* during the early war years, and had instructors who were often experienced pilots, including some of the combat veterans from the *Legion Condor*.

In effect, training was an on-going process. This was because of changing tactical situations caused by, for example, different operating environments and the calibre of opponent likely to be met in a new campaign. It was also necessary for pilots to be versatile in being able to transition onto new aircraft types. In the case of the Bf 109, pilots who were conversant with the Jumo-engined 'Dora' had to work hard to move onto the 'Emil', with its very different and more powerful DB 601-series engine.

Even at frontline unit level, lectures and briefings were common on tactics and combat. These were often made by the most experienced pilots, rather than the highest-ranking. Within the Luftwaffe there was generally a camaraderie amongst personnel regardless of class or social position that was very different to pre-war forces such as the RAF. This even extended to the close relationship

Oberstleutnant Werner Mölders indulges in some 'hangar flying', while Oberstleutnant Adolf Galland (left) and Generalmajor Theodor Osterkamp (right) look on. The occasion was a party in April 1941 to celebrate Osterkamp's 49th birthday, which was on the 15th of that month. (Author's Collection)

between pilots and their groundcrews. The latter were generally known as 'black men' due to their smart, dark-coloured overalls, and it was not uncommon for a pilot to be on first-name terms with his ground personnel. Such a relationship was similar to that which existed later in the war between USAAF pilots and their groundcrews.

When it came to the use of tactics, however, in practice it was often up to the individual pilot's skill and ability to improvise that set apart German aviators from many of their opponents in the early war period. This was partly due to training, and also through a thorough know-how of the capabilities and performance of the Bf 109s that they flew.

During the opening months of the war, in fighter-versus-fighter encounters, it was found that all too often enemy formations simply scattered in all directions, with apparently no tactical awareness. Certainly the concept of the wingman, which had become so important in German combat doctrine, was often not adhered to by other nations, even though it was seemingly known about and acknowledged by many. It took the numerous bitter lessons of the *Blitzkrieg* era for the Allies to realise the importance of the type of tactical thinking that the Germans had in effect invented for aerial warfare in the late 1930s and during the early stages of World War II.

This completely played into the hands of the *Jagdflieger* in 1939–40. It soon became an accepted procedure to 'bounce' enemy fighter formations out of the sun, make a rapid firing pass to scatter their opponents, and then climb back to altitude ready to make another diving attack. The second pass would obviously be more complicated because the enemy fighters were now more scattered and less easy to pinpoint, and the initial element of surprise had been lost. But the enemy pilots would also be disorientated and potentially easier to shoot down the second time around.

However, the *Jagdflieger* were also well aware that some of the Allied fighters they faced could out-turn the Bf 109 in a close-in dogfight. For this reason the Germans were again able to employ a feature of the Bf 109 that was so useful in combat. If they themselves became the victim of a 'bounce', a means of escape was to turn into the attacker and roll over inverted or near inverted and then dive away. This used the Bf 109E's fuel-injected DB 601 engine to advantage, because it would continue to run smoothly during such a manoeuvre. In contrast, some Allied fighters did not have this advantage. The Rolls-Royce Merlin engine in the Hurricane, for example, featured a carburettor system that was likely to cut out, and so lose the initiative due to momentary fuel starvation.

As a last resort, the Bf 109 could be put into a roll followed by a steep dive at full or near to full power, but the pilot had to ensure that there was sufficient altitude to safely perform this manoeuvre because a considerable amount of height could be lost very quickly. Such a tactic was known to the Americans as a 'Split-S', and it was used by the USAAF later in the war – it appears to have been known as an *Abschwung* to the Germans.

This 'text book' *Schwarm* features Bf 109Es of 8./JG 26 'Schlageter' on a training flight from Essen-Müleim in early 1940. The formation is led by 'White 1', with all four pilots leaning forward in their cockpits looking out for one another. (Author's Collection)

The Luftwaffe fighter units that formed in the time up to and during the *Blitzkrieg* period also held another key element that was a part of the overall make-up of the *Jagdwaffe*'s inventory of resources. This was an esprit de corps that stemmed partly from units being associated with a particular area or conurbation near to their home airfield.

The most successful fighter *Gruppe* of the Polish campaign, JGr 102, had close links with the town of Bernburg where the unit was originally formed. Indeed, its fighters carried a caricature of the 'Hunter of Bernburg' on their fuselage sides. It became a popular story at the time that during the fighting in Poland, when JGr 102 had moved forward to a Polish airfield to keep up with the advances on the ground, its personnel received a very welcome gift – several crates of beer, sent specially on the orders of the *Bürgermeister* of Bernburg and flown in by a Luftwaffe transport aircraft. This type of morale boost was a godsend to pilots who were fatigued by combat flying and had little chance of rest until a campaign was won.

The *Schwarm* or four-aircraft formation became the classic Luftwaffe fighter combat tactic, itself comprising two elements of two fighters (*Rotte*). Werner Mölders had a major hand in developing this procedure, which was based on combat experience in Spain and replaced the previous rigid 'parade-ground' rules which were inappropriate for modern aerial combat. The RAF was much slower to realise the benefit of this arrangement, sticking to the rigid vic and line astern formations for the Battle of France and much of the Battle of Britain. However, it too eventually adopted the 'finger-four' formation. In this image, four Bf 109Es from III./JG 51 fly in a *Schwarm* for the camera. (Author's Collection)

CHAPTER 6
COMBAT

The defeat of Poland in such a rapid and thorough way demonstrated the overriding success of the new type of warfare that the Germans had adopted. Thenceforward, *Blitzkrieg* was to become the main platform of Germany's method of waging war until the tide turned against the Wehrmacht later in World War II.

It had been a considerable worry for the military planners in Berlin during the autumn of 1939 that the western Allies (Britain and France) would actively intervene on the ground as well as in the air by aiding Poland with an all-out assault on Germany's western border. The fact that so many *Jagdwaffe* units were kept in that part of Germany even while the Polish campaign was taking place amply demonstrated this concern. In the event there was no such intervention by Britain and France, and the 'western front' settled into a period that has taken on the name 'Phoney War' in English parlance, 'Drôle de Guerre' in French and *Sitzkrieg* (literally 'sitting down war') for the Germans.

However, none of these terms were at all appropriate for the personnel on both sides who opposed each other, for although there was very little fighting on the ground, there was much activity in the air. The winter of 1939–40 was a particularly harsh one in northern Europe, but even so there was a gradual escalation of aerial fighting that led to losses on both sides.

With the victory well and truly sealed in the east over Poland, the Luftwaffe was able to increasingly concentrate almost all of its fighter assets in western Germany to face the French, who had also declared war on 3 September hours after Britain's similar action. There was a movement westwards of existing units, including those that had participated in the Polish campaign. In addition, further *Gruppen* were established, and many *Geschwader* were brought up to full strength with the creation of a proper *Stab*. In this way the Germans once more used a lull in activity to further strengthen frontline capability, in similar fashion to the way in which the period of peace following the Munich Crisis had been a time of considerable reorganisation and successful rearmament for the Luftwaffe.

A significant development within the ranks of the *Jagdwaffe* units in the weeks and months following the ending of the Polish campaign was the gradual

withdrawal of the Jumo-engined Bf 109D from frontline day fighter units, and its replacement by the Bf 109E. Henceforth, only makeshift nightfighter units and training schools were the main home of the 'Dora'. Thus, by the time of the Battle of France in May 1940, only elements of JG 27 were still flying Jumo-engined Bf 109s, and then only for a short time until the 'Emil' reigned supreme within the ranks of the single-engined day fighter units for much of the remainder of 1940.

Increasingly, the cannon-armed Bf 109E-3 replaced the all machine gun-armed Bf 109E-1. And starting to come into service during the spring and early summer of 1940 was the E-4, with its uprated cannon armament and various detail improvements that made the Bf 109 an even more potentially deadly opponent for those facing it.

The *Sitzkrieg* on the 'western front' initially involved sporadic aerial action between German warplanes and a variety of French-operated aircraft. This mainly took the form of dogfights in the vicinity of the Franco-German border between *Jagdwaffe* Bf 109s and *Armée de l'Air* Morane-Saulnier MS.406s and US-supplied Hawk H-75 fighters.

Probably the first victory in the west was achieved on 8 September 1939 when a two-aircraft *Rotte* of Bf 109Ds from II./JG 52 came across and shot down a slow French reconnaissance aircraft, thought to be either a Mureaux 115 or 117. The victorious pilot was Leutnant Paul Gutbrod.

That same day the *Jagdwaffe* suffered a loss that could have been much more serious for the Germans. A *Schwarm* of Bf 109Es from I./JG 53 tangled with several Hawk H-75s of GC II/5, with one of the Messerschmitts subsequently making an emergency landing during which it overturned. Fortunately for the Luftwaffe, the pilot escaped, albeit with back injuries. He was none other than Hauptmann Werner Mölders, the highest-scoring *Legion Condor* pilot in Spain and the architect of much that the Luftwaffe was learning about good

Although based at Wiesbaden-Erbenheim when German troops invaded Poland on 1 September 1939, elements of I./JG 53 dispersed to a meadow away from the airfield as a precautionary measure against possible enemy air attacks. (Tony Holmes Collection)

fighter tactics. The dogfight that resulted in his crash was a salutary lesson for Mölders and his colleagues that even with well-disciplined tactical awareness, the enemy might still be able to gain the upper hand.

On 20 September the situation was reversed when Mölders, recovered from the back injury caused by his crash, was able to shoot down a Hawk H-75. He was amongst several pilots that would go on to become high-scoring *Experten* (aces) who achieved their first successes of the war during that period while flying the Bf 109. One was Gefreiter Heinz Bär of I./JG 51, who shot down a Hawk H-75 on 25 September for the first of his 208 victories, many of these being claimed while flying Bf 109s of several different versions. Another was Leutnant Helmut Wick from I./JG 2 based at Frankfurt-Rebstock, who shot down a Hawk H-75 on 22 November. He gave the following description of the action to the Luftwaffe magazine *Der Adler*:

Because the French did not cross our [German] border very often, my wingman and I decided for once to pay them a visit. Near Nancy I suddenly saw a gaggle of aircraft at an altitude of around 6,000m. Realising immediately that they were not German, we began to circle. Two aircraft detached themselves from the bunch above and swooped down on us. Now I could recognise them – Curtiss fighters.

We dived away and, just as we had anticipated, the two Frenchmen dived after us. I went into a climbing turn, with one of the Frenchmen right on my tail. I can still clearly remember how I could see his red, white and blue roundels when I looked behind me. At first, the sight of them was rather exciting, particularly as the Frenchman was firing away with everything he had. But then the realisation that somebody is behind you and shooting at you becomes very unpleasant.

I pushed the nose down again and, with my superior speed, quickly lost him. When my Frenchman was no longer to be seen, I looked up to my left to find the others. Not a thing in sight. I glanced up to my right and could hardly believe my eyes. I was staring at four radial engines coming at me all sprouting little red flames. A ridiculous thought flashed through my mind – 'Are they really allowed to shoot at me like that?' But then I was all concentration. Should I try to get away again? No! Now's the time to tackle them. One of them has got to go down. Clenching my teeth, I hauled the stick and rudder to the right and turned into them.

By the time I had completed my turn the first Curtiss had already shot past me. The second was right behind him, and this one I attacked head-on. It was a nasty moment looking straight down his blazing gun barrels, but we were too close to score any hits. He zoomed over my head and now the third one was almost on top of me. I manoeuvred my aircraft slightly to get him nicely lined up in my sights, aiming and firing just as I had been taught at fighter training school. With my first shots I saw some pieces of metal fly off the Frenchman. Then both his wings buckled and gave way. Close behind him, the fourth Curtiss was also firing at me, but I was not hit.

The first pair were now climbing again. I followed suit so that they could not catch me. I was getting low on fuel and it was already time to head for home. My wingman, who had returned to base safe and sound, had lost me after the first dive in all the twisting and turning.

A pensive Leutnant Helmut Wick of 3./JG 2 was photographed at the unit's Frankfurt-Rebstock home shortly after he had claimed the *Geschwader*'s first victory over the 'western front' on 22 November 1939. His tally had risen to 56 by the time he was killed in combat on 28 November 1940. (Tony Holmes Collection)

Apparently bored by 'Phoney War' inactivity, two Luftwaffe personnel played football, while in the background several groundcrew 'black men' manhandle a Bf 109E-1 of I./JG 77 beneath a makeshift and rather flimsy-looking camouflage arrangement. The location was possibly Odendorf, home to I./JG 77 for several months up to the start of the Battle of France. (Author's Collection)

Wick's Hawk H-75 was the first of 56 victories he would be credited with in the west prior to his death in combat with RAF Spitfires on 28 November 1940 off the south coast of England.

The opening encounters on the 'western front' did not include RAF aircraft, but shortly after the commencement of hostilities the British Army and RAF began moving assets to France as the British Expeditionary Force (BEF). Initially, RAF squadrons equipped with Hurricanes came under the BEF umbrella in its Air Component within No 60 (Fighter) Wing. The Hurricane was a type that the German pilots had not encountered before.

A second RAF element known as the Advanced Air Striking Force (AASF) was also sent to France as quickly as possible. At first the latter was made up entirely of Battle light bombers from No 1 Group, Bomber Command, which were subsequently joined by Blenheims of No 2 Group. But when these started taking losses while operating unescorted, two of the fighter squadrons of the BEF were seconded to the AASF as No 67 (Fighter) Wing.

The first significant combat between Bf 109s and Hurricanes took place on 22 December 1939, when two of three No 87 Sqn aircraft were shot down and their pilots killed after being 'bounced' by a *Schwarm* of Bf 109Es from III./JG 53 led by the increasingly celebrated Hauptmann Werner Mölders.

This type of encounter was, however, comparatively rare. The short range and endurance of the fighters on both sides resulted in there being few major clashes between the Hurricanes and their opposing Bf 109s, the British fighters and their German counterparts tending instead to engage with longer-range light bombers, reconnaissance and army co-operation aircraft flying near to their own airfields. The Hurricane in fact gave as good as it got when the two types of fighters did meet during the 'Phoney War', and in the German-versus-French encounters there were often successes for both sides.

Amongst the most serious dogfights for the *Jagdwaffe* occurred on 6 November 1939, when JGr 102 had a deadly encounter with Hawk H-75s of GC II/5. Led by Major Johannes Gentzen, this *Jagdgeschwader* had been the most successful fighter unit during the Polish campaign, and had since moved west to a new base at Lachen-Speyerdorf. Still equipped with Bf 109Ds, its pilots were about to discover that the 'Dora' was now outclassed by far better fighter opposition than had been encountered over Poland.

While attempting to intercept a French Potez 63 reconnaissance aircraft escorted by nine Hawk H-75 fighters, no fewer than 27 'Doras' became embroiled in a series of individual skirmishes that resulted in four Messerschmitts being shot down and four more damaged and their pilots forced to crash-land. Gentzen himself was credited with one of the Hawk H-75s to bring his personal score to eight, but it was clear that the planned replacement of the Bf 109D by the Bf 109E or, in the case of Gentzen's *Gruppe*, by the Bf 110C, was overdue and needed addressing at once.

As the 'Phoney War' continued, a growing number of *Jagdwaffe* units became operational on the 'Emil', especially the 20mm cannon-armed E-3, and successes against both British and French aircraft started to increase. The appearance of the Bf 109E-3 gave the Germans a considerable increase in firepower compared to the machine gun-armed British and French aircraft that they were encountering, making the Bf 109 the most potent fighter by far on the 'western front'.

One of these encounters featured the often very busy JG 53 and, specifically, Oberleutnant Heinz Bretnütz, who was a veteran of combat over Spain with the *Legion Condor*. He had served with 2.J/88 in the closing months of 1938 and into early 1939, during which time he was credited with two aerial victories. On his return to Germany, he was posted to Bf 109E-equipped JG 53. Joining 6. *Staffel*, he was its *Staffelkapitän* from August 1939 to October 1940, when he became *Gruppenkommandeur* of II./JG 53.

One of the most active *Jagdwaffe* units during the *Blitzkrieg* period was JG 77. Serving in both the Polish and French campaigns, the *Geschwader* was also present for the Norwegian invasion by way of its II. *Gruppe*. In this image, Bf 109E-1s of I./JG 77 were photographed prior to the Battle of France if the image's official caption is to be believed, probably at the *Gruppe's* pre-*Fall Gelb* base at Odendorf. (Author's Collection)

Oberleutnant Heinz Bretnütz of 6./JG 53 claimed eight victories during the 'Phoney War' and the Battle of France. He followed this up with a further 17 kills through to the end of November 1940, by which point he had become *Gruppenkommandeur* of II./JG 53. Bretnütz is seen here wearing the Knight's Cross of the Iron Cross and full overwater rig of lifejacket and a high-visibility yellow helmet cover. The additional pilot armour, just visible behind his head in the sideways-opened cockpit canopy, was introduced on the Bf 109E-4 and retrofitted to some earlier 'Emils'. (Author's Collection)

JG 53 was one of the Luftwaffe fighter units to be fully involved in frontline operations during the 'Phoney War', particularly in its aerial defence of the vital Saar area of the border, and its pilots were often dogfighting in skirmishes with French fighters. Bretnütz made his first aerial victory claim of World War II

1555 hrs, 31 MARCH 1940

NEAR SAARGEMÜND

1 Pilots from II./JG 53 flying a mid-afternoon patrol at 12,000ft near Saargemünd spot a formation of MS.406s from GC III/7 below them. Among the German pilots is Oberleutnant Heinz Bretnütz at the controls his beloved Bf 109E-3 'Yellow 10'. The Messerschmitts are in a *Schwarm* formation, developed from experience of combat over Spain, while the French formation is loose and undisciplined.

2 The Bf 109Es attack in *Rotte* pairs, hitting the MS.406s in classic 'boom and zoom' passes, using their speed and superior performance to climb back above the shocked French pilots before making another diving pass.

3 With the GC III/7 formation in disarray, the Bf 109E pilots continue with their attacks, hitting the evading and increasingly scattered MS.406s from every angle.

4 Unable to offer any cohesive resistance, three of the Moranes are shot down in flames and two more are destroyed in forced landings. Bretnütz himself is credited with two victories.

FOLLOWING PAGES

Peter was the smart Bf 109E-3 'Yellow 10' flown by Oberleutnant Heinz Bretnütz of 6./JG 53 during the 'Phoney War' and Battle of France period. On 31 March 1940, flying from Mannheim-Sandhofen, Bf 109Es of II./JG 53 entered a dogfight with MS.406 fighters, Bretnütz shooting down two of the French aircraft. Asleep on the 'Emil's' wing is one of the unit's 'black men' groundcrew. (Author's Collection)

on 25 September 1939, when he was credited with shooting down a Hawk H-75 fighter near Bienwald.

On 31 March 1940, he was flying as a part of a patrol with other members of II./JG 53, operating from the unit's long-time base at Mannheim-Sandhofen. The formation of Bf 109Es was led by the *Gruppenkommandeur*, Hauptmann Günther Freiherr von Maltzahn. They encountered several MS.406s of GC III/7 and a major dogfight developed. As was increasingly the case while the 'Phoney War' continued, the French fighters were flown in a disorganised manner that suggested a lack of tactical awareness. In total, the German pilots made claims for six of the French Moranes destroyed, with II./JG 53's success reflecting the growing ascendency of the 'Emil'-equipped units on the 'western front'. Bretnütz was credited with shooting down two of the Moranes near Saargemünd to record his fourth and fifth victories.

On 9 April 1940 Germany launched Operation *Weserübung* – the invasion of Denmark and Norway. Denmark capitulated very rapidly, but the fighting in Norway eventually lasted for two months. As far as the *Jagdwaffe* was concerned, only the increasingly well-travelled JG 77 with its Bf 109Es was involved in the single-engined fighter operations to support the campaign. Indeed, only II./JG 77 was committed to the actual fighting, its personnel operating alongside the Bf 110Cs of ZGs 1, 26 and 76. Opposed by a motley collection of biplanes and other totally outclassed types such as Royal Navy Skuas, they successfully gained and held aerial supremacy, allowing other Luftwaffe assets and the German ground and naval forces to finally prevail against stubborn Allied resistance in Norway.

Eventually it was the western theatre which was to see by far the most action of the first nine months of World War II. The *Blitzkrieg* unleashed by the Germans on 10 May 1940 against the Low Countries and France was the ultimate expression of the successful execution of the 'lightning war' theory. Under the code name *Fall Gelb*, a simultaneous attack was launched that very quickly overwhelmed the Netherlands and led to the Allies being drawn into a fatal trap while trying to go to the aid of the rapidly beleaguered Belgians. The related main German attack further south through the Ardennes to commence the sweep into France was unnamed, but it was the ultimate key to the whole operation. The overall plan depended on air and ground resources working closely together in a similar blueprint to the successful campaign against Poland but on a much larger scale and with many more potential opponents.

For the *Jagdwaffe*, two whole *Luftflotten* were involved, with much greater strength than the two *Luftflotten* that had been committed to the Polish operations. These were *Luftflotte* 2 (commanded by *General der Flieger* Albert Kesselring), covering the northern part of the intended war front, and *Luftflotte* 3 (*General der Flieger* Hugo Sperrle), delegated to the southern area. Both had a sizeable number of Bf 109E-equipped *Geschwader* attached. Official figures vary, but according to most recently accepted totals, up to 1,016 Bf 109s were committed to the start of the *Fall Gelb* operations.

However, within the Luftwaffe's unit organisation, any frontline *Staffel* or *Gruppe* could be temporarily assigned to another *Geschwader* as demanded by the tactical situation. Therefore, not all *Geschwader* were 'together' as cohesive units for the 10 May attack, but their roles remained roughly the same as executed during the Polish campaign. They were to support the Wehrmacht units on the ground, help suppress enemy opposition particularly by neutralising its aerial assets (both on the ground and in the air) and gain and hold supremacy in the air.

To that end, virtually all the *Jagdwaffe* and its Bf 109Es were committed to the campaign in the west. The only units not present for action or potential use in support of *Fall Gelb* were the elements of JG 77 that were fighting in Norway and local defence units held back in Germany itself. The most important of the latter was the *Stab* and II. *Gruppe* of JG 3, which were stationed at Zerbst specifically to provide defensive air cover for Berlin.

In addition to the fighter units assigned to *Fall Gelb*, the Luftwaffe also committed fully equipped *Gruppen* of Bf 110C *Zerstörer*, Ju 52/3m transports, dive-bombers and conventional bombers. The latter had been gradually moved into place in the weeks leading up to the start of the operation, the fighter units already being largely in their desired locations due to their prolonged action over the 'western front' during the previous months. Overall, this enormous show of strength and potential numerical superiority in the west gave the whole plan a viability that was not lost in the subsequent persecution of the attack.

The *Jagdwaffe*'s Bf 109E units were in action as soon as the execution of *Fall Gelb* commenced in the early hours of 10 May. It was *Luftflotte* 2's fighters that duly bore the brunt of the initial air activity. Amongst the first units in action were elements of München Gladbach-based JG 27, which began covering the Ju 52/3m transports from just after 0500 hrs local time as they ferried paratroopers charged with seizing the strategically important Albert Canal.

Oberleutnant Dieter Robitzsch's Bf 109E-1 'Black 1' of 5.(J)/TrGr 186 sits forlornly on the grass at De Kooy airfield after it was forced down by D.XXI pilot Lt Henk J van Overvest of 1e JaVa during the surprise attack on the Dutch base on 10 May 1940. (Tony Holmes Collection)

Aerial combat with a miscellany of totally outclassed warplanes followed, but the achievement of surprise meant that on this first day many opposing air assets were destroyed on the ground by the Luftwaffe's bombers. One of the first aerial victories was achieved by Leutnant Hans-Ekkehard Bob of I./JG 21 (attached to JG 27) who brought down a Belgian Gloster Gladiator for his first claim. In such encounters the Bf 109E was in theory the easy victor, but a level of flying skill was needed to slow the Messerschmitt down sufficiently to fire at the antiquated biplane while maintaining safe flying speed and manoeuvring in whatever way was necessary at the same time.

Hans-Ekkehard Bob was one of many *Blitzkrieg*-era *Jagdwaffe* personnel who continued to fly and fight during the later stages of World War II, eventually seeing combat in Me 262 fighters with JV 44. He would survive the conflict with 57 victories to his name.

The following day saw the first claims made during the Battle of France campaign by the pilot who would emerge as the *Jagdwaffe's* top-scorer in that phase of the war. Hauptmann Wilhelm Balthasar of I./JG 1, who had flown in Spain with the *Legion Condor* and was therefore already an experienced combat pilot with seven (some sources quote six) victories. On 11 May he was credited with four kills – three Belgian Gladiators and a French MS.406.

This early phase of the campaign drew in a diverse mix of Allied fighters from Belgium, the Netherlands, France and Britain. But the overwhelming nature of the air and ground war unleashed by the Germans very rapidly saw these nations having to wage a defensive campaign in which the Netherlands was the first to fall after only a brief period of fighting.

One of the *Jagdwaffe* units that was involved in the fleeting action over the Netherlands was II.(J)/TrGr 186. This *Gruppe* had played a small part in the Polish campaign, after which it had been immersed in the defence of the north German coast, particularly over the German Bight, for most of its time while flying the Bf 109. In the opening months of 1940 this had been a comparatively quiet part of the air war, but the unit achieved its first aerial victory on 27 February with the destruction of an RAF Blenheim that was undertaking an armed reconnaissance of the area.

However, II.(J)/TrGr 186 was a major participant in the early actions of *Fall Gelb*, with its pilots enjoying success over the Netherlands. Tasked with covering the Dutch coastline and preventing any air activity from that area interfering with the main German attacks further inland, the unit's pilots became embroiled in combat with Dutch Fokker D.XXI fighters of 1e JaVa (*Jachtvlieg Afdeling* – fighter squadron) based at De Kooy airfield near the naval base of Den Helder in the northwest of the Netherlands. This unit had 11 operational fighters at the time of the invasion, and they fought several engagements with Bf 109s.

In total, the pilots of II.(J)/TrGr 186 claimed eight aerial victories on 10 May. One of the successful pilots was Oberfeldwebel Kurt Ubben, who achieved his first kill. He was eventually credited with 93 confirmed victories and 13 unconfirmed prior to his death in combat with USAAF fighters on 27 April 1944.

0450 hrs, 10 MAY 1940

DE KOOY NAVAL AIR STATION

1 Following a frustrating dawn patrol that saw 11 D.XXIs of 1e JaVA fail to engage much faster Bf 109Es off Texel Island, the pilots return to De Kooy Naval Air Station, north of Amsterdam, to refuel. With their comrades providing top cover, 'Kleuter' Flight comes in to land.

2 As 'Kleuter' Flight roll out on the grass runway, they are 'bounced' by at least two *Schwärme* of Bf 109Es from 5.(J)/TrGr 186. D.XXI '241' flown by Lt Jan Bosch crashes in flames. Lt Focquin de Grave, flying '218', takes off again, while '219', flown by Lt Henk J. van Overvest zooms upwards as the Messerschmitts scream past them, strafing ground targets.

3 As the D.XXI top cover dives in to attack, the Bf 109Es use their superior speed to fly wide circles and mount slashing attacks against the slower but more manoeuvrable Fokker fighters.

4 The Bf 109E-1 of Oberleutnant Dieter Robitzsch is hit by fire from van Overvest as it crosses in front of him, leaving a long trail of glycol streaming behind the mortally damaged Messerschmitt.

5 With de Grave flying beside him, Lt Robert van der Stok, in '234', turns into the fight and catches a Messerschmitt as it turns across his path. Leaving a white trail, the German fighter dives away and heads east.

6 A second Bf 109E comes in from the left, but van der Stok turns sharply to engage it.

7 The Bf 109E and van der Stok begin a turning fight, making three full circles before the superior turn rate of the Fokker puts it behind the Messerschmitt.

8 Realising the threat from behind, the German pilot (probably Unteroffizier W. Rudolf) veers to the right, but the move places him directly in the centre of van der Stok's gunsight.

9 Hit hard by fire from van der Stok's D.XXI, the Bf 109E starts trailing oil and glycol as it initially zooms upwards, before falling away in a spin.

10 With ammunition running low and their limited endurance starting to be stretched, the Messerschmitt pilots disengage and head east for home. Several are seen to be trailing smoke as they depart, while the Bf 109E of Unteroffizier Rudolf crashes in Den Helder. Having been badly wounded in the engagement, Rudolf passes away in captivity on 14 May.

11 As the battle-damaged D.XXIs come in to land at De Kooy, Leutnant Robitzsch has no choice but to force-land beside them and surrender.

FOLLOWING PAGES

In reply, the Dutch Fokker pilots achieved a number of victories of their own. During a dogfight in the vicinity of De Kooy airfield, Lt Henk J van Overvest succeeded in shooting down the Bf 109E flown by Oberleutnant Dieter Robitzsch. The German pilot successfully belly landed his disabled Messerschmitt onto the airfield itself and was taken prisoner. He was duly removed to Britain and then transported to Canada, where he remained for the rest of World War II.

The rapidly escalating war on the 'western front' immediately led to many deadly encounters taking place on a larger scale than had occurred during the 'Phoney War'. These almost at once resulted in combat between the *Jagdwaffe*'s Bf 109Es and their counterparts from the RAF and the *Armée de l'Air*. With the Dutch and Belgian fighters virtually annihilated in the opening days of the conflict either through aerial combat or more often due to bombing and strafing of their airfields, it was up to the British and French to try to hold the line in the air against the increasingly successful Germans.

Unfortunately for the Allies, the swift German advances led to desperate measures. In particular, it became necessary almost straight away to destroy several key bridges, especially those near Maastricht. The only means to do this was to use the light bombers of both the RAF and, initially, the Belgian Air Force (French aircraft were also subsequently involved). These missions led to dramatic losses of firstly Belgian-operated Battles, followed a day later (on 12 May) by those of No 12 Sqn, RAF.

Flying escort and top cover for these vulnerable light bombers also proved to be a dangerous undertaking. As noted in Chapter 3, on the 12th, Hauptmann Adolf Galland achieved his first aerial victories when, flying with his fellow pilots from *Stab* JG 27, he helped to break up a formation of Hurricanes from No 87 Sqn that were flying top cover for Blenheim light bombers engaged in the bridge attacks. JG 27 easily scattered the Hurricane escort and Galland downed two of the RAF fighters for his first aerial victories.

The fighting in the north effectively 'sprung' the trap that drew British and French forces into Belgium, leaving their rear areas exposed to attack from the

JG 2 inflicted significant losses on Allied aircraft during the Battle of France, with its I. and II. *Gruppe* being credited with 16 victories on 10 May alone. Ten days later, the *Geschwader* passed the century mark since the beginning of the *Blitzkrieg* in the west, and by the time JG 2 made its last claim of the Battle of France on 15 June, its tally had reached 185 victories. The unidentified pilot flying 8./JG 2's 'Red 9' during the spring of 1940 has four victory bars adorning his tailfin. (Tony Holmes Collection)

south. In the following days the southernmost of the German forces successfully pushed through and out of the Ardennes, cutting off Allied ground forces and isolating the Channel ports. This led to renewed attacks on communications targets – especially bridges – with disastrous results.

For the *Jagdwaffe* pilots, 14 May was 'the day of the fighters', as they enjoyed an overwhelming victory over the light bombers of the RAF which failed in their objectives of attempting to halt the German advance over the River Meuse. Contemporary totals suggest that Allied losses that day were 89 light bombers and fighters, with JG 53 being particularly successful. Oberleutnant Hans-Karl Mayer, *Staffelkapitän* of 1./JG 53, was credited with five victories, making him one of several Luftwaffe 'aces in a day' from the early war years. Mayer was a veteran of the *Legion Condor* in Spain, and his success again underlined the importance of pre-war combat experience combined with the excellence of the Bf 109E as a fighter.

The Netherlands capitulated on 14 May, and although the Belgians succeeded in hanging on for a further two weeks, by that time the situation was completely hopeless for the Allies.

Not all the accomplished exponents of the Bf 109E during the successful German campaign were new recruits. The Luftwaffe continued to retain in its higher echelons a cadre of experienced officers, some of whom had taken part in World War I. Amongst these was Oberst Theodor 'Theo' Osterkamp, the highest-scoring German naval fighter pilot of that war, who was one of the most experienced senior officers of the Luftwaffe in a combat role. As the *Geschwaderkommodore* of JG 51, he led by example and was fully involved in the fighting firstly over the Netherlands and then northern France. Amiable, well liked and respected by his men, 'Onkel Theo' as he was affectionately known achieved several aerial victories during the campaign that commenced on 10 May.

As German ground forces forged ever deeper into northwestern France, former *Armée de l'Air* airfields became available for use, allowing *Jagdwaffe* units to vacate their bases in western Germany and move nearer to the frontline. This was particularly important for units flying Bf 109Es due the fighters' comparatively limited endurance. One of those finding excellent new accommodation was JG 53, whose 2. *Staffel* moved into Charleville alongside elements of JG 27. Sometimes, however, such a forward deployment was premature, as was discovered by I./JG 77 when it moved to Escarmain on 20 May. Within hours of arriving, the airfield was subjected to a counter-attack by 400 heavily armed French infantrymen.

The largest aerial battles of the whole *Blitzkrieg* period took place in the skies over the Dunkirk area as British and French forces were withdrawn by sea in Operation *Dynamo*. The latter took place between 26 May and 4 June, with the main part of the evacuation ending on the 3rd. The troops being shipped back to England were under often constant bombardment from the air, principally during the hours of daylight.

Dynamo was also the first occasion in which the Bf 109E *Jagdflieger* met large numbers of Spitfires in aerial combat. Although they had been held back from much of the fighting over France, Spitfire units based in southeast England were fully involved in covering the Dunkirk evacuation. It was the first significant occasion when Spitfires and Hurricanes flew together against the Luftwaffe.

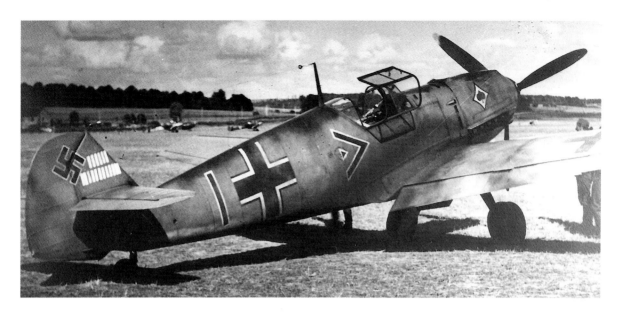

The uniquely marked Bf 109E-3 of Hauptmann Werner Mölders during the Battle of France. It is high likely that he was shot down in this aircraft on 5 June 1940 by the D.520 of Sous-lieutenant René Pomier-Layrargues of GC II/7. At that time Mölders was *Gruppenkommandeur* of III./JG 53. The fuselage of his suitably marked 'Emil' was over-sprayed with a dull coat of grey, probably RLM 02 Grau. (EN Archive)

Hauptmann Werner Mölders proudly wears the Knight's Cross of the Iron Cross awarded to him on 29 May 1940 for becoming the first German fighter pilot to achieve 20 victories in World War II. His victories are well documented, so it remains a mystery as to why there are only 18 marked on the tailfin of his machine seen here. One suggestion is that this is Mölders' reserve Bf 109E which did not yet display the two victories he achieved northwest of Amiens on 27 May 1940 (Tony Holmes Collection)

The fighting over the Dunkirk area also saw some dogfights between Bf 109Es and the unconventional Boulton Paul Defiant turret fighter. But whereas combat with Spitfires was a portent of what was to come in the following months over southern England, the Defiants enjoyed only a brief foray in the frontline as a day fighter before its career in that unforgiving arena ended prematurely later that summer. As soon as the *Jagdwaffe* pilots had become accustomed to the unusual layout of the Defiant it became easier to deal with this unconventional fighter, especially as the aircraft did not have a fixed forward-firing armament.

Several Bf 109E pilots were also able to get the better of Spitfires in a number of increasingly frantic encounters. One of them was Hauptmann Adolf Galland, who claimed a Spitfire on 2 June just as the Dunkirk fighting was reaching its climax. At that time was still flying with *Stab* JG 27. Interviewed after the war, Galland pointed out, 'Although slower than our Me 109s, the Spitfire was a good adversary. They fought hard over Dunkirk. They made every effort to help the evacuation. We had some of our most dangerous moments of the war over the Dunkirk beaches.'

It was a point that was echoed by Günther Rall, who was then a Leutnant with III./JG 52. The future third highest-scoring Luftwaffe fighter pilot of World War II with 274 victories had admiration for the Spitfire, which he felt was the greatest threat posed to the Bf 109's mastery of the air at that time. 'The British were sporting. They would accept a fight under almost all conditions. We preferred to see from our cockpits Hurricanes or Frenchmen, not Spitfires!'

RAF light bombers were also engaged during the Dunkirk evacuation, as Adolf Galland recounted in *The First and the Last:*

On 29 May I flew a sortie with the staff flight in this [Dunkirk] sector. We spotted a formation of British Blenheim bombers below us. Two of them were shot down and crashed into the sea. The second one escaped me for some time by skilful evasive action, until low over the water my bullets ripped open her oil tank. She hit the water at a shallow angle and sank immediately. When I landed at Saint-Pol, I found that my Me 109 was covered with oil.

The Dunkirk operations left a lasting memory for Galland and his colleagues:

During the embarkation of the British troops thick clouds of smoke lay over the battlefield. The huge stores of fuel and war materiel had been set on fire. As number 1A of our wing, it was my duty to fly the aircraft on our commander's flank. Oberstleutnant [Max] Ibel had been a pilot in World War I. This gruff Bavarian was very popular with us. He was no longer a youngster, and the energy with which he tried to keep up to date with modern fighter aircraft and flying called for the greatest respect.

I flew with him that day through the thick grey-black clouds of smoke, which rose to a great height, when suddenly a wing of Spitfires dove on us. We both saw them

One of the highest-scoring *Jagdwaffe* pilots in terms of victory claims during the Battle of France was Oberfeldwebel Werner Machold of 1./JG 2 'Richthofen'. In this posed publicity image, he was photographed painting a victory bar onto the rudder of his Bf 109E. Credited with ten aerial victories during the fighting over France, he was shot down on 9 June 1941 while attacking British warships off Portland, in Dorset, and became a PoW. (Author's Collection)

Hauptmann Wilhelm Balthasar was the highest-scoring Luftwaffe *Jagdflieger* during the Battle of France, with 23 claims and a number of strafing 'victories'. Already an ace from his combat activities in the Spanish Civil War, he flew with I./JG 1 and was awarded the coveted *Ritterkreuz* in June 1940. Balthasar, who subsequently became *Geschwaderkommodore* of JG 2, had increased his score to at least 38 victories in the West by the time he was killed in action dogfighting with Spitfires of No 609 Sqn on 3 July 1941. (Tony Holmes Collection)

at the same time. Almost simultaneously we warned each other over the intercom. However, we reacted differently, which normally should not have happened, since I was supposed to accompany the other aircraft. I saw my commander vanish in the smoke, and prayed that he might escape unscathed. I singled out a British pilot, blazing away with all I had, not seriously expecting much more than a strengthening of my slightly battered self-confidence. The Spits roared past me, tailing my commander, sure of their target. I could not find him again. He did not return with the others to Saint-Pol, our base. We were already really worried when late at night he arrived on foot. The Spitfires caught him, but he had managed to get away with a lucky crash landing.

The evacuation of RAF fighter assets from France itself began prior to the end of May, while the *Armée de l'Air* continued fighting with its antiquated MS.406 and Bloch MB.152 fighters – both types were completely outclassed by the Bf 109E-3 and the better-armed and armoured E-4. The latter 'Emil' started to arrive in numbers for *Jagdwaffe* units during the late spring and early summer of 1940.

By then a sizeable number of D.520s had entered service, this new French fighter proving a match for the Bf 109E-3. Nevertheless, it was too late to be of any influence on the overall outcome of the Battle of France. Tragically for the *Armée de l'Air*, many of its best pilots lost their lives in the frantic air battles that took place in May–June 1940. Sheer weight of numbers, the element of surprise, experience and better equipment allowed the Luftwaffe to very quickly gain command of the skies and never to lose it.

Undoubtedly successful in many encounters, the Bf 109s did not by any means have matters all their own way. This was now a total war in every sense of the word, and the Battle of France was the first time that the Bf 109 had been confronted in large, daily air battles by fighters that were in key parameters its equal. RAF Hurricanes and newly arriving D.520 fighters were a match for the Bf 109E, although they could not better the cannon armament of the established Bf 109E-3 and the new E-4.

Commencing on 3 June, Operation *Paula* was launched with the aim of finally defeating the *Armée de l'Air*. Specific military targets, including airfields, were also attacked, although by that late stage of the campaign it was highly likely that most French aerial opposition was going to be disorganised and piecemeal.

The overwhelming success of *Fall Gelb* leading to the military disasters culminating in the evacuation from Dunkirk, together with the taking of much of northeastern France, allowed *Fall Rot* (Case Red or Plan Red) to be commenced on 5/6 June. The Wehrmacht's mechanised ground units, again supported by overwhelming air power, were able to rapidly advance both eastwards and southwards into the heart of France, confirming the overall French defeat.

Despite being close to capitulation, the *Armée de l'Air* continued to take the fight to the *Jagdwaffe* as best it could. Galland clashed with French aircraft on several occasions, including on 9 June:

I had just shot down an unidentified aircraft similar to a Curtiss, when we – I was flying with Hauptmann [Albrecht von] Ankum-Frank – encountered two flights of Moranes. There was an incredible dogfight.

'Ace in a day' Oberleutnant Hans-Karl Mayer (third from left) and pilots of his 1. *Staffel* enjoy the sun at Douzy during the brief hiatus between Operations *Fall Gelb* and *Fall Rot*, the two-part conquest of France. The French campaign was very much the calm before the storm for 1./JG 53, with five of these pilots subsequently being either killed or captured in the seven weeks from late August to mid-October 1940. They are, from left to right, Leutnant Alfred Zeis (PoW from 5 October 1940), Unteroffizier Heinrich Höhnisch (PoW from 9 September 1940), Oberleutnant Hans-Karl Mayer (killed on 17 October 1940), Leutnant Ernst-Albrecht Schulz (survived), Unteroffizier Herbert Tzschoppe (PoW from 15 September 1940) and Feldwebel Heinrich Bezner (killed on 26 August 1940). (Tony Holmes Collection)

The only thing to do was to attack first and then try to escape as best we could. I closed in on the tail-end aeroplane and banked still steeper! The fellow flew well, but his aircraft was inferior to mine. At last, from a short distance, I managed to get in a broadside on a climbing turn. He burst into flames. I avoided him only by inches. I bent a blade on my propeller and the right astern against his wing. My aerial was shaved off: it had been about three feet long. The Morane spun down in flames and crashed into a forest not far from Meaux, north of Paris.

No time to lose! I closed in on the next one! Well riddled, she went vertically down with a black smoke trail. I could not observe the crash because the rest of the Moranes were harassing me, so I could not register this kill. It would have been my 13th.

In the final days of the Battle of France, there was renewed competition for the accolade of highest-scoring *Jagdwaffe* pilot. But with Hauptmann Werner Mölders a temporary PoW, the easy winner was eventually Hauptmann Wilhelm Balthasar of I./JG 1, who was credited with 23 aerial victories.

Freed from most aerial activity, the Bf 109 pilots were able to assist the overall effort by strafing French airfields and army units. Anti-aircraft fire was patchy, sometimes effective, but often non-existent due to the disorganised French retreat.

On 20 June, III./JG 53 was given the honour of providing air cover over the Forest of Compiègne where negotiations were taking place leading to an armistice and the total capitulation of France. The armistice was signed on 22 June, to come into effect three days later. This represented the total defeat of France, and it was the most substantial triumph of the *Blitzkrieg* era – an overwhelming victory that had been achieved with lightning speed. The *Jagdwaffe* units equipped with the Bf 109E had played a massive part in the whole military operation, ensuring aerial supremacy and allowing mechanised forces to complete their task with a speed that not even the Wehrmacht's military commanders could have believed.

Subsequent to the end of the fighting in France, there was a major redirection in the role of the Luftwaffe's combat units. Initially, the Bf 109E *Geschwader* were tasked with 'defending' the territory that had been conquered from outside interference. To that end some of the *Jagdwaffe*'s Bf 109E units underwent a major relocation exercise. Several were moved into parts of France that had not seen any fighting but were of course fully included in the final armistice settlement. JG 53, for example, moved across the country to airfields in Brittany, that part of northwest France now conquered and a source of airfields for controlling the western approaches to both France and Britain. The *Stab*, I./JG 53 and III./JG 53 moved into the airfield at Rennes, with II./JG 53 taking up residence at Dinan.

Elsewhere, newly occupied airfields in Belgium and the Netherlands were to be the home for Luftwaffe units – a situation that was only rectified following the D-Day landings on 6 June 1944 and their subsequent recapture by the Allies.

For the time being, however, there would be a short lull in the air war following the defeat of France, during which time the *Jagdwaffe* units were able to regroup, welcome new pilots and briefly rest their combat veterans. But by early July the next major offensive was shaping up to take place – the Battle of Britain.

AFTERMATH

The Bf 109 was thoroughly combat tested, and proven, firstly in the Spanish Civil War and thereafter during the *Blitzkrieg* period of the opening months of World War II. It subsequently grew into being one of that conflict's most iconic warplanes. Bf 109s duly served on all fronts during the war over Europe, North Africa and the Mediterranean, and more than 33,000 examples of the type were eventually built in a multitude of variants. This made it one of the most widely produced aircraft of that conflict, indeed of all time. It also remained in service after the war ended for a handful of operators around the world, including Czechoslovakia, Israel and Spain, and flew in combat during various smaller but no less deadly conflicts. The Bf 109 was one of the few warplanes that was already well established in frontline service at the start of World War II, and it was still being used with great success at the end of the conflict.

Immediately following the defeat of France in June 1940, 'Emils' served in the much more difficult Battle of Britain. This proved to be the most deadly

A line up of Bf 109Es and Fs of IV./*Ergänzungsgruppe* JG 3 probably at Monchy-Breton during the late spring of 1941. The *Gruppe* supplied a small number of Bf 109F-2s to its *Stab*, 1. *Einsatzstaffel* (Operational Training Squadron) and 2. *Schulstaffel* (Training Squadron), although the bulk of the aeroplanes flown by the tyro fighter pilots assigned to the unit were war-weary 'Emils'. JG 3 headed east for Operation *Barbarossa* shortly after this photograph was taken. (EN Archive)

combat that the Bf 109 had known up to that time compared to the relatively easy actions in Spain, Poland, the Low Countries and France. Operating at the very limits of its range, and faced by modern fighter opposition that was often located in the right place for interception due to Britain's excellent radar infrastructure, the Bf 109E at last met its match – although it was never entirely beaten. Instead, the type increasingly flew not just as a pure fighter, but also as a fighter-bomber (*Jabo*) as well; a role that the Bf 109 made its own during the coming years.

The Bf 109E was joined at the frontline by the more powerful Bf 109F from October 1940 onwards. The 'Friedrich' was considerably altered (it at last successfully featured a centrally mounted cannon), and the aircraft proved to be the match of contemporary Allied fighters. It served with notable success in North Africa and the Soviet Union. Continuing development led to the Bf 109G, which was a mainstay of the Luftwaffe's day fighter force during the mid and latter stages of World War II alongside the Focke-Wulf Fw 190. However, by that time weight increases, the growing superiority of Allied fighters and a shortage of trained and competent pilots had started to seriously degrade the Bf 109's effectiveness. The final major production model was the late-war Bf 109K, a very capable fighter that was nonetheless unable to help stem the tide of overwhelming Allied superiority in the air.

The Bf 109 was flown by the three top-scoring fighter aces of all time. Credited with the incredible total of 352 aerial victories, Major Erich Hartmann of JG 52 is (and always will be) the highest-scoring fighter pilot in the history of air warfare, and his mount was the Bf 109.

The tactics that were used by the Luftwaffe's *Jagdflieger* during the *Blitzkrieg* period were revolutionary. In effect, modern aerial warfare commenced during the Spanish Civil War using (what were then) state of the art fighters, and it was therefore a proving ground not just for the Bf 109, but for a new type of aerial combat. Particularly due to developments pioneered by expert aviators including the charismatic Werner Mölders, the Bf 109 swept virtually all before it over Spain and subsequently achieved similar results right up to the end of the *Blitzkrieg* period in June 1940. In particular, the four-aircraft *Schwarm* formation of two pairs that had first been successfully tried out by the Luftwaffe's *Legion Condor* during the Spanish Civil War was developed into a highly effective tool in the *Blitzkrieg* era. When its benefits became obvious, the formation was rapidly adopted as the 'finger-four' by the RAF, and proved to be a useful asset during the Battle of Britain for both sides.

Indeed, the tactics developed and honed to perfection by the Luftwaffe over Spain and then by Bf 109 pilots during the opening months of World War II had a lasting effect on aerial warfare, and continued to be used long after the *Blitzkrieg* period had ended. Even in the post-war jet age, the concepts still held great importance.

SELECTED SOURCES

Bekker, Cajus, *The Luftwaffe War Diaries – The German Air Force in World War II* (Ballantine Books, New York, 1975)

Galland, Adolf, *The First and the Last* (Methuen, London, 1955)

Holmes, Tony, *Osprey Aircraft of the Aces 18 – Hurricane Aces 1939-40* (Osprey Publishing, London, 1998)

Laureau, Patrick, *Condor – The Luftwaffe in Spain, 1936-1939* (Hikoki Publications, Ottringham, 2000)

Marchand, Patrick, and Takamori, Junko, *Les Ailes de Gloire No.6 – Curtiss Hawk 75* (Editions d'Along, Le Muy, France, 2001)

Marchand, Patrick, and Takamori, Junko, *Les Ailes de Gloire No.8 – Dewoitine D.520* (Editions d'Along, Le Muy, France, 2002)

Mombeek, Eric, *Jagdwaffe – The Spanish Civil War (Luftwaffe Colours Volume One Section 2)* (Classic Publications, Crowborough, 1999)

Mombeek, Eric, *Jagdwaffe – Blitzkrieg and Sitzkrieg, Poland and France 1939–1940 (Luftwaffe Colours Volume One Section 3)* (Classic Publications, Crowborough, 1999)

Mombeek, Eric, *Jagdwaffe – Attack in the West May 1940 (Luftwaffe Colours Volume One Section 4)* (Classic Publications, Crowborough, 2000)

Morareau, Lucien, Stenman, Kari, et. al., *Le Morane-Saulnier MS 406 – Collection Histoire de l'Aviation No.5* (Lela Presse, Outreau, France, 2002)

Price, Alfred, *Luftwaffe Handbook 1939-1945* (Ian Allan, Shepperton, 1977)

Stedman, Robert, *Osprey Warrior 122 – Jagdflieger – Luftwaffe Fighter Pilot 1939-45* (Osprey Publishing, Botley, Oxford, 2008)

Ullmann, Michael, *Luftwaffe Colours 1935-1945* (Hikoki Publications, Aldershot, 2002)

Weal, John, *Osprey Aircraft of the Aces 11 – Bf 109D/E Aces 1939-41* (Osprey Publishing, London, 1996)

Weal, John, *Osprey Aviation Elite 1 – Jagdgeschwader 2 'Richthofen'* (Osprey Publishing, Botley, Oxford, 2000)

Weal, John, *Osprey Aviation Elite 12 – Jagdgeschwader 27 'Afrika'* (Osprey Publishing, Botley, Oxford, 2003)

Weal, John, *Osprey Aviation Elite 22 – Jagdgeschwader 51 'Mölders'* (Osprey Publishing, Botley, Oxford, 2006)

Weal, John, *Osprey Aviation Elite 25 – Jagdgeschwader 53 'Pik As'* (Osprey Publishing, Botley, Oxford, 2007)

Official Technical Manuals for the Bf 109, including *L.Dv. 228/1: Messerschmitt Bf 109B* (August 1937); *D.(Luft) T.229/4: Messerschmitt Bf 109E* (July 1940); *L.Dv.T 2404/Bo: Messerschmitt Bf 109E* (March 1941)

Transcripts and notes from interviews with former Luftwaffe personnel, including interview text from the John Batchelor archive.

INDEX

Page numbers in **bold** refer to illustrations and their captions.